Sew It Easy
With
Fleece &
Flannel™

Edited by Jeanne Stauffer

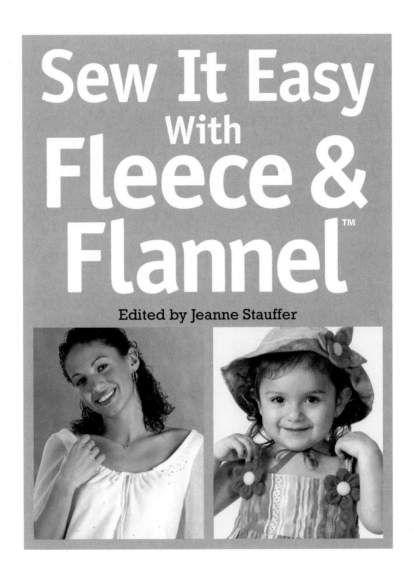

HOUSE of
WHITE
BIRCHES

PUBLISHERS
SINCE 1947

SEW IT EASY WITH FLEECE & FLANNEL

EDITOR	Jeanne Stauffer
MANAGING EDITOR	Barb Sprunger
TECHNICAL EDITOR	Mary Jo Kurten
COPY EDITORS	Michelle Beck, Nicki Lehman
	Conor Allen
PHOTOGRAPHY	Tammy Christian, Christena Green,
	Kelly Heydinger
PHOTOGRAPHY STYLIST	Tammy Nussbaum
PRODUCTION COORDINATOR	Brenda Gallmeyer
GRAPHIC ARTS SUPERVISOR	Ronda Bechinski
ART DIRECTOR	Brad Snow
BOOK DESIGN	Brad Snow, Ronda Bechinski
GRAPHIC ARTISTS	Ronda Bechinski, Jessi Butler
PRODUCTION ASSISTANT	Marj Morgan
TRAFFIC COORDINATOR	Sandra Beres
TECHNICAL ARTISTS	Liz Morgan, Chad Summers
CHIEF EXECUTIVE OFFICER	John Robinson
PUBLISHING DIRECTOR	David J. McKee
BOOK MARKETING DIRECTOR	Craig Scott
EDITORIAL DIRECTOR	Vivian Rothe
PUBLISHING SERVICES DIRECTOR	Brenda R. Wendling

Printed in the United States of America
First Printing: 2004
Library of Congress Number: 2003108835
ISBN: 1-59217-038-2

Welcome

You'll love sewing with today's fleece and flannel fabrics. They come in a rainbow of colors, and they're so easy to work with. If you haven't sewn with them recently, you are in for a wonderful surprise. They are no longer just for pajamas.

Once you take a look at the projects in this book, you'll realize that fleece and flannel can have an upscale, fashionable look when

used in the right designs. Combined with suede, a touch of gold braid or a series of tucks, you'll find wearables in this book that are ready for a night on the town.

If you like to celebrate, flannel and fleece can create the look you want for your home as well, giving it a special holiday flair. If you just want the comfy, at-home look, fleece and flannel can do that better than any other fabrics.

They are both soft to touch, drape easily and provide just the right amount of warmth for any weather. You'll also find lots of soft, cuddly projects for babies and toddlers in this book, along with a special section of guidelines and tips for sewing with these fabulous fabrics.

So, welcome to Sew It Easy With Fleece & Flannel. Come in and enjoy the fun activity of deciding which project to stitch first. You'll be surprised how quickly you can stitch a project made with fleece or flannel!

Warm regards,

CONTENTS

A TOUCH OF CLASS

SOFT HOLIDAY ACCENTS

COMFY AT HOME

CUDDLE ME BABY

Indulge in the softer side of

sewing with wonderful, cozy fleece and flannel fabrics. Gone are the limited colors, stiff flannels and pilling fleeces of yesterday. Today's fabrics are available in a delightful rainbow of solid colors, prints and plaids designed to appeal to every taste, in weights and qualities to suit myriad fabrications and priced to please any budget.

These exciting fabrics have also traveled far beyond the flannel shirt and pajamas or basic fleece jacket. They've joined the ranks of traditionally higher-end fabrics, keeping company with them in upscale ready-to-wear fashions and trendy home decor accessories. And why not? Everyone loves them and it's easy to see why. They're so versatile—soft and cozy to the touch and warm to wear, making them equally perfect for baby, Grandma and your teenage son. For the home, they're luxurious for cuddling and adaptable to any decorating style ranging from country to contemporary.

Throughout the pages of this book, you'll find projects for fleece and flannel that take these fabrics to new heights. Whether you're looking for adorable gifts to make for baby, clever holiday accents for your home, upscale decorating ideas or fashions ranging from sleepwear to evening wear, the perfect idea is here waiting for you. And more good news—these fabrics are easy to sew, making them suitable for seamstresses of any age or skill level. You may even entice your child to sew with a trendy project like the fun-loving Teen Pajama Pants & Top on page 88. In fact, you're likely to find that

Soft Sweet Shirt

the only difficult thing in this book is deciding what to make first.

FLANNEL

Characteristics and Selection

Most commonly made of worsted, woolen or cotton fibers, flannel can also be made with rayon or manufactured fibers. These soft and warm fabrics are woven with either a plain or twill weave and are lightly napped to raise the fiber ends on one or both sides. Flannel fabric features a dull finish and is available in a variety of weights ranging from light to heavy. It is often preshrunk.

Like flannel, and often referred to as flannel, flannelette fabric is soft and warm and woven with a twill or plain weave. However, flannelette is always made of cotton and is usually napped on only one side. Flannelette also has a dull finish and is available in light to medium weights. It is usually preshrunk.

Generally speaking, wool flannel is often used for suits, coats, shirts, dresses and jackets, while cotton flannel and flannelette are commonly selected for shirts, infant and children's wear, sleepwear, quilts and home decor accessories. However, the best type of flannel or flannelette to select depends on what you're making, the fabric characteristics you desire, the look you want to achieve and the durability needed. Medium and heavier weights are generally more durable than very light weights and offer more stability, but very heavy weights are bulky and more difficult to ease or shape. Fabrics napped on both sides will usually be thicker and softer than those napped on only one side and more suitable for garments, quilts and other projects where stability is desired.

For garments, worsted flannel is more tightly woven, lighter in weight, has a more visible weave and is more wear-resistant than wool flannel, while wool flannel is softer and fuzzier. Wool flannel will be easier to press and warmer than cotton flannel, but may also require dry-cleaning to maintain its good looks, while cotton can be machine washed. Because cotton fibers are shorter than wool fibers, cotton flannel tends to shed more lint and pill more than wool flannel. All flannel fabrics tend to show wear in garment areas subject to friction and tend to sag unless they are underlined.

As with any fabric, quality counts, and this is especially true with flannel. A high-quality flannel will be much easier to sew, stretch less, appear more attractive and feel softer and warmer than a lesser grade. A finished project made with a good flannel fabric will be more durable, maintain its shape and general appearance better and pill less than one made with an inferior fabric. Before purchasing a flannel or flannelette fabric, examine it carefully. No matter what the weight, a high-quality fabric will have a thick,

Kid's Kimono

soft nap and a hand that feels pleasing to the touch. A lower quality fabric may appear thin, stretchy and flimsy. Also beware of a heavily sized fabric that may distort excessively when the sizing is washed out; to determine heavy sizing, rub a folded section of the fabric between your fingers and look for a powdery residue, or observe if the fabric is noticeably softer. If the fabric has a printed or woven design, check to make sure the design is fairly straight on the grain. The weave should also appear straight and even. Fabric with a distorted weave is difficult to cut evenly, stretches excessively when sewn and may distort even more after your project is completed. Another test is to hold the fabric up to the light to observe evenness in the weave; a loose weave is characteristic, but if thin areas are obvious, it's either woven too loosely or unevenly. The best words of advice: run from inferior fabrics—your time is too precious to waste sewing with anything that will give you less than successful results.

FLANNEL

Flower Bright Jumper

Autumn Leaves Throw

Pattern and Project Selection When

selecting the best pattern or project to use with a flannel fabric, consider the fabric's fiber content and weight. For example, wool flannel, especially worsted wool, is easier to press and holds a crease better than cotton flannel, making it suitable for a variety of tailored or pleated styles.

Cotton flannel and flannelette fabrics are loosely woven and fray easily. For best results, choose patterns or projects without small or intricate pieces that will be difficult to work with without fraying, or plan to stabilize the pieces with fusible interfacing before cutting. For quilts and other pieced projects, it's easiest to work with large basic shapes.

Very lightweight flannel or flannelette fabrics are suitable for garments or projects that will not receive harsh wear or abrasion. They are a good choice for making soft gathers or creating a more delicate look.

Medium flannel weights are suitable for a wide range of garments and projects and offer the most versatility.

Heavy flannels are ideal for garments and projects where durability, weight and a bulkier look are desired. Choose patterns that require a minimum of easing or gathering.

Because flannel shrinks and prewashing is recommended, purchase 1/4 yard more than required for the pattern or project.

Preparation
For the best results, preshrink flannels twice before cutting. In addition to preventing shrinkage in the finished garment or project, preshrinking tightens the weave and raises the nap to make the fabric even softer. The exception to the preshrinking rule is for quilters who desire an old-fashioned look with the fabric puckered at seam and quilting lines.

For wool flannel that will be dry-cleaned after fabricating, have a dry cleaner pre-shrink the yardage for you. For cotton or wool flannels that will be machine washed after fabricating, prewash using a gentle machine cycle, cool water and a mild soap. Be careful not to over-load the machine and do not use fabric softener. Machine dry at a low to medium temperature. Press the fabric using a dry iron if needed, be-ing careful not to stretch it as you press; do not use steam as it will stretch the fabric. If desired, use spray sizing when you press the fabric to give it more stability.

Cutting
Cut flannel using scissors or a rotary cutter; a rotary cutter is especially ideal for long edges that may stretch when cutting with scissors. Use a "with nap" layout and pin closely to prevent stretching. Be especially careful not to distort the fabric when cutting on the bias. If you're making a garment, quilt or other project that usually requires a 1/4-inch seam allowance, increase the seam allowance to 3/8 inch or 1/2 inch to allow for fraying; this will help prevent the seams from pulling apart. If fraying or stretching is a concern on small or detailed

pieces, fuse lightweight interfacing to the wrong side of the fabric before cutting out the pieces; this will also prevent distortion when cutting curves and diagonal lines on the bias.

Sewing
Sewing flannel is easy, but some flannels stretch more than others and you need to take care to prevent stretched seams. For the best results, follow these tips:

- Pin pieces together before stitching, placeing pins close together to avoid stretching the edge.
- Use a size 80 or 90 universal needle, depending on the flannel weight. Because flannel will dull the needle quickly, begin with a new needle and replace it when it appears to be dull.
- Use cotton thread in the needle and bobbin for stitching seams. For quilting or decorative topstitching where you want the stitches to show, use a 40-weight or other heavier thread to avoid the stitches blending into the flannel nap.
- Use at least a 3/8- or 1/2-inch seam allowance.

Eggs-ceptional Place Mat

- If the flannel you're stitching tends to shift with a regular presser foot, use a walking or even feed foot.
- Press seams open as you sew, using a dry iron.
- Finish seam allowances and raw edges with serging, zigzag stitches or binding.
- Sewing flannel creates a lot of lint. Stop stitching and clean under your machine throat plate frequently.
- Avoid ripping seams—ripping tends to stretch the seam line and fray the seam allowances. If you must rip, use a sharp seam ripper and try not to pull on the seam as you remove the stitches.
- Use interfacing when making buttonholes. Apply seam sealant such as Fray Check to the stitched buttonhole before cutting it open.
- To bind the edges of quilts, place mats or other layered flannel projects, use extra-wide purchased binding such as fleece binding or cut your bias strips a little wider than usual to accommodate the loft of the fleece. If you're using very stretchy flannel, consider cutting the bias binding strips from coordinating cotton broadcloth instead of the flannel.

Just For Fun Thanks to the fuzzy, fraying nature of flannel, it readily lends itself to decorative techniques like fringing and frayed seams on the right side of a project.

To fringe the edge of flannel, first determine the length you'd like to make the fringe—usually 1 inch to 2 inches. Mark a line this distance from the fabric edge. Using a medium to short stitch length, stitch along the marked line. Clip the fabric to the stitching line at 1-inch intervals. Remove the crosswise threads between the clips.

For outside seams with a fuzzy appearance, sew the pieces wrong sides together using a $3/8$-inch to $1/2$-inch seam allowance. Wash the pieced fabrics to fray the seam allowances. If you want to reduce the threads and fuzz in your washing machine, follow the fringe instructions to fringe the seam allowances before washing.

FLEECE

Characteristics and Selection
Fleece is a lightweight, yet warm, comfortable fabric that's durable and strong. It doesn't rip or tear easily, ravel or shrink. Fleece can be single or double-sided and is usually made with polyester fibers that are first twisted into yarns, then knitted into a base fabric and dyed or printed. The knitted fabric is brushed with wire brushes to compact the fabric and give it a soft, fuzzy surface that's sheared and finished. The resulting fabric is warm and wind-resistant—the brushing creates insulating air pockets that keep warmth in and cold out, and the compacted fibers resist wind. Because polyester naturally repels water, fleece is also hydrophobic, or water-resistant, and it wicks moisture away from the body to keep you dry. Lower qualities of fleece have a tendency to pill, while

Fluffy Fleece Bathrobe

FLEECE

high-quality fleece fabrics have low-pilling qualities. Fleece is available in light, medium and heavy weights in a wide range of colors, prints, finishes and qualities.

Like flannel, fleece qualities vary, and using a high-quality fleece will give you a much better sewing experience and ensure successful results. High-quality fleece fabrics are made from closely knit, high-quality yarns that are sheared and veloured multiple times to reduce pilling and increase durability. High quality fleeces are resilient and often have special low-pilling or water-repellant finishes.

When selecting fleece, look for a thick, dense fabric with a lofty nap that feels good to the touch and doesn't show the threads beneath. A flimsy feel or threads showing through the nap indicate a thin, loosely woven fabric that was poorly napped.

Because fleece is a knit, its resiliency is also an indicator of good quality. It should recover to its original dimension smoothly and quickly when you stretch it and let it relax; if it ripples or stays extended it won't maintain its shape after sewing either.

To estimate the fabric's durability, rub it vigorously against itself on each side of the fleece—if it loses its shape, pills or appears rough, the quality is inferior and it will not wear well.

If the fleece has a printed design, make sure the design lines are clear and printed fairly straight on the grain.

Pattern and Project Selection

When selecting the best pattern or project to use with a fleece fabric, consider the fleece weight and how the garment or project will be used. Many commercial garment, accessory and home decor patterns are specifically designed for use with fleece and are an excellent choice. They offer features like flatter sleeve caps on garments and simple lines that work well with fleece fabrics. Because fleece is bulky and non-raveling, some fleece patterns feature $1/4$-inch seam allowances instead of $5/8$ inch. Generally, you want to choose patterns that have a dropped sleeve or flatter sleeve cap that doesn't require easing, don't require a lot of easing, have fairly simple design lines without intricate details, and a relaxed fit. Also keep in mind that it's easier to add zippers than buttonholes for fleece closures.

For a lighter-weight fleece, choose garment patterns for indoor wear or projects where the bulk and warmth of heavier fleece isn't needed or desired. It's especially ideal for garments that will be worn close to the body and for infant's wear and pajamas.

Medium-weight fleece is the most versatile and widely available weight. It's suitable for a wide range of indoor wear or outerwear garments for every age, totes, scarves, hats, mittens, pillows, throws and other home decor accessories.

Snowflake Warmer Set

Heavyweight fleece is excellent for outer-wear and offers optimal benefits against the elements with its characteristics that keep you warm, dry and protected from wind. Use it for shirts, jackets, coats, scarves, hats and gloves.

Because fleece doesn't ravel or fray, it's highly suitable for garments and projects with unhemmed edges that are cut straight or decoratively, easy appliqués, layered designs and cut out reverse appliqué techniques. It's also easy to cut into fringe and novelty shapes. However, it will stretch out of shape if used for single-layer ties. For projects with ties, plan to stitch a doubled fleece tie or use ribbon.

Getting Started
Because fleece doesn't shrink, there's no need to prewash the fabric before cutting and sewing.

Although fleece can be single-sided, it's most often double-sided. It's important to determine which side of the fleece is the right side and to mark the pieces diligently so you're using the same side as the right side for every piece. Unlike other fabrics with obvious right sides, with double-sided fleece it isn't that apparent at first glance. You do want to figure it out, though, because the right side of the fabric will maintain its appearance and wear better than the wrong side. If you look at the cut edge of some heavyweight fleeces, one side will appear thicker than the other; the thicker side is the right side. This can often be difficult to discern on medium or lighter weights, and it's more accurate to determine the right side by pulling the fabric. Usually, fleece will curl to the wrong side when a cut edge is pulled on the cross grain (across the fabric width) and to the right side when pulled along the lengthwise grain or selvage. Once you've determined this, mark the wrong side of each piece with a chalk marker or a pin right after you cut it out.

Fleece projects usually don't need interfacing, but if you do, use tricot or other knit interfacing.

Layout and Cutting
Fleece does have a nap, and it's more noticeable on some fabrics than others. If you rub your hand along the surface lengthwise in each direction, you'll notice that one direction will feel smoother than the other; the color may also appear slightly darker when the nap is rubbed in one direction. Although either direction can be used, on some fleeces the color will look nicer and it will wear better when the nap is going down. Just like the right side, it's important to pick a direction and stick with it for every piece. For example, if your jacket fronts and back are cut with the nap running one direction and the sleeves are cut with the nap running the opposite direction, they may appear to be two different shades of the fabric color when the jacket is sewn together.

For cutting, place the fabric on a flat surface

Royal Diamond Pintucks Jacket

FLEECE

where it won't hang over an edge and stretch, possibly distorting the pattern pieces. An extra-large cutting mat designed for home decor fabrics works especially well for cutting out fleece. If you're using a purchased pattern, follow the "with nap" layout in the instructions. For all other projects, lay out all pieces in the same direction. Extra-long pins with bead heads are easiest to use with the thickness of the fleece, and the bead heads won't get lost in the nap. Use a chalk marker to make any necessary pattern markings.

Cut the fleece pieces using scissors or a rotary cutter and mat. A large 60mm rotary cutter is especially ideal for cutting thick fleece, and when used with a clear quilter's ruler will give you very straight, accurate edges. Be sure to hold the rotary cutter perpendicular to the surface and not at an angle to ensure accuracy. If you experience difficulty cutting doubled fleece layers, cut the pieces from each layer separately.

Pressing
Pressing isn't recommended for fleece. Finger pressing is usually sufficient for seams. If you simply must press a seam, hold the iron above the surface and steam it, then finger-press or use a press cloth. Use a press cloth and light pressure to fuse tricot-knit interfacing in place if it's needed. Never place an iron directly on fleece. It can melt the fabric or leave a permanent mark.

Sewing and Serging Basics
Like flannel, sewing with fleece creates a lot of lint. Whether you're using a sewing machine or serger, be sure the machine is clean and oiled before you begin. Be sure to stop frequently and remove the lint from under the machine throat plate and around the needle. Because the lint soaks up machine oil, also stop and follow your machine manual to clean and oil it if you're doing a lot of sewing or serging with fleece.

Thread
Use good quality polyester thread that matches the fabric or is a shade darker. Use a new stretch, universal or ballpoint needle.

Needles
For basic sewing, select a size 70/10 needle for lightweight fleece, size 80/12 or 90/14 for medium to medium-heavy weights and size 100/16 for very heavy outdoor weights. It's best to use the smallest size needle, but if it skips stitches or breaks or bends when you stitch, use the next size larger. You will also need to use a larger size for stitching areas with more than two layers of fabric. Special considerations must also be taken when combining fleece with fabrics like faux suede or leather. Fleece expert Nancy Cornwell suggests selecting your needle according to the "fussiest" element of your sewing, whether it's a fabric or specialty thread. For example, use a stretch needle for faux suede and a leather needle for leather, since they are "fussier" than the fleece. All synthetic fibers dull needles quickly, so change to a new needle when it appears necessary.

Stitch Length and Machine Settings
Follow these tips for successful fleece sewing and serging:

- Use a longer stitch length for fleece than you would for other fabrics. A too-short stitch length will result in puckered or ruffled seams. Use 7–9 stitches per inch, or 3mm to 4mm stitch length, adjusting as needed to adapt to the fabric depth. For seams that will receive a lot of stress and need strength, use the shortest possible length that will still result in a smooth seam. Test on fabric scraps to determine the best stitch length for the fleece you're using.
- Sew slowly, being careful not to stretch the fleece as you sew. Stitches are difficult to remove, so it's better to take your time and stitch accurately the first time.
- If seams still pucker with a longer stitch length, slightly reduce the presser foot pressure.
- Sometimes fleece tends to "pile up" in front of the presser foot instead of feeding smoothly

under it. If this occurs, use the tip of a seam ripper, point turner or small scissors (anything to compress it—except your finger) to flatten the fabric as it goes under the foot.

- The best serger stitch is a four-thread overlock. If you use a three-thread overlock stitch, reinforce the stitching line with a conventional sewing machine.
- If needed for flat seams, adjust the differential feed to 1 or 1.5.
- A sharp cutting blade is essential for serging fleece. If the blade is dull, it will chew doubled fleece edges rather than cutting them, resulting in lumpy, uneven seam allowances.
- Self-adhesive, double-sided basting tape is a great alternative to pins when working with fleece. This holds edges securely and straight for myriad tasks, including positioning pockets, zippers or appliqués, hems and lapped seams.

Seam Options

Seam options vary, depending on the seam allowance width you're using. Serge a basic seam or sew it and finger-press the seam allowances open.

Because fleece doesn't ravel, the raw edges of seam allowances, facings and hems don't need to be finished. For raw edges that will show, it looks nice to finish them with pinking shears, a rotary cutter with a decorative blade, serging or zigzag stitches.

For unruly seam allowances or decorative effects, also consider some of the following seam ideas.

Topstitched seams. For a $5/8$-inch seam allowance, finger-press the seam allowance open. Topstitch in place $1/4$ inch from the seam line on each side. For a $1/4$-inch seam allowance, finger-press the seam allowances to one side and topstitch close to the seam line.

Lapped seams. A lapped seam reduces bulk and adds an attractive, decorative look. The edges to be lapped should be cut with a rotary cutter to be straight and blunt. This technique can be used with any width seam allowance;

Wreath Pillow

purchased fleece patterns may include $5/8$-inch or $1/4$-inch seam allowances, depending on the pattern company.

Using double-sided basting tape on the upper layer, overlap garment pieces from the front to the back. For a $5/8$-inch seam allowance, overlap the edges $1\,1/4$ inches; for a $1/4$-inch seam allowance, overlap the edges $1/2$ inch. Sew the layers together close to the upper layer edge, then $1/4$ inch from the edge. Trim any excess fabric from the lower layer.

Mock flat-felled seams. This seam finish gives the seam an attractive look on the wrong side. Sew the seam with a $5/8$-inch seam allowance. Trim one seam allowance only to $1/8$ inch, finger-press the other seam allowance over it and topstitch close to the edge.

Right-side seam allowances. Seam allowances on the right side of a garment add a sporty, novel look. Sew the seam with wrong sides together, using the seam allowance width of your choice. Trim the seam allowances evenly with a rotary cutter and straight or decorative blade.

FLEECE

Edge Finishes

Edge finishes abound for fleece. Choose the finish that best suits the style of your garment or project and fleece weight.

Unbound single-layer edges. Because fleece won't fray or ravel, single-layer edges can be left plain and decoratively cut, topstitched or embellished by stitching braid, ribbon or novelty trim along the edge. You can also serge the edge with decorative rayon thread or Woolly Nylon thread.

A hand-stitched blanket stitch is another attractive finish for a single-layer edge. To ensure stitches spaced evenly from the edge, machine baste the desired width from the edge. Use lightweight yarn to sew the blanket stitches, then remove the basting threads.

Bound single-layer edges. A bound edge is an attractive look that's often seen on ready-to-wear. For a designer look, bind the edges with Lycra binding strips, fleece binding, fold-over braid, double-fold bias tape, wide ribbon or faux suede strips.

Ribbing. Depending on the garment style, ribbing is a good edge finish for hems, cuffs and some necklines. Purchase precut ribbing or make your own by cutting it from interlock knit fabric.

Traditional hems. To finish an edge with a traditional hem, turn the edge under 1/2-inch and topstitch close to the edge.

Closures

Snaps, buttons and buttonholes or loops, zippers and ties are all good closure options for fleece.

Snaps. Large, decorative snaps look especially nice when used for a fleece closure. Apply stabilizer to the wrong side of the fabric before attaching the snaps to prevent them from pulling out of the fabric.

Buttons. Buttons can be used with buttonholes or loops made of ribbon, suede, leather or doubled fleece.

Care must be taken with buttonholes to prevent the fabric from distorting and the stitches from sinking into the nap. To stitch buttonholes, pin a piece of water-soluble stabilizer on the fleece right side and a piece of tear-away stabilizer on the wrong side at each button placement. Mark the buttonhole on the water-soluble stabilizer and stitch as usual. The stabilizers prevent the stitches from sinking into the fabric nap and keep them smooth and even; the tear-away stabilizer on the wrong side prevents the fabric from stretching as you stitch. After completing all buttonholes, rinse to remove the water-soluble stabilizer and carefully pull the tear-away stabilizer from the stitches. Use tear-away stabilizer on the wrong side only, because some stabilizer may remain and show through the stitches.

As an alternative to stabilizing the buttonhole on both sides, you can stitch buttonholes through faux suede patches for a decorative effect. For each buttonhole, cut a patch of suede

Ready for Travel Jackets

slightly larger than the buttonhole. Secure the patches to the right side using basting tape and place tear-away stabilizer on the wrong side. Mark the buttonhole on the suede and stitch as usual. Tear away the stabilizer after completing the buttonholes.

Zippers. Wide-teeth sport zippers are most often used on fleece. To avoid wavy zippers, work on a flat surface. Apply basting tape to the zipper tape and press the zipper firmly into place on the seam allowances, being careful not to stretch the fleece. Sew the zipper in place using a longer stitch length.

Just For Fun

Fleece lends itself beautifully to myriad creative techniques, many of which are featured throughout the pages of this book. Following is a sampling of some of these techniques.

Applique. Faux suede is an ideal appliqué for fleece. Simply secure it in place with basting tape and topstitch close to the edges.

Pumpkin Pullover

Cutwork and Reverse Applique. Cutwork is easy to do on fleece because the edges don't ravel. Use basting spray to adhere a design pattern to be stitched around or trace the design onto water-soluble stabilizer and pin it to the fleece for stitching. Cut out the area inside the stitching. Two layers can be stitched together to create a reverse appliqué effect. See the Child's Pumpkin Pullover on page 73 and the Snowflake Winter Warmer on page 116.

Decorative Stitches and Embroidery. Decorative stitches and machine embroidery are popular fleece embellishments and easy to add. Use water-soluble stabilizer on the right side of the fleece and tear-away stabilizer on the wrong side.

Fringe. It's easy to cut fringe along a fleece edge when you use a rotary cutter, clear acrylic ruler and cutting mat. Place the fleece flat on the mat, lining up the edge with a marked mat line. Use the clear ruler and rotary cutter to cut fringe in the desired width and length, using the mat lines as a guide for keeping the ruler straight. See the Snowflake Winter Warmer on page 116.

Sculpting. Decorative or heavyweight threads create a sculpted effect when stitched across the surface of fleece. Use water-soluble stabilizer on the surface when stitching to prevent the stitches from getting lost in the nap. See Sculpted Fleece Pajamas on page 36 and Out 'n' About Jacket on page 24.

Fleece Care

To launder fleece, turn garments inside out to reduce pilling and wash only with other fleece items. Use powdered detergent and wash on a gentle cycle in cool to lukewarm water. Do not use liquid detergent or fabric softener. Hang to dry or machine-dry on a short cycle at a low temperature, being careful not to over-dry. Dry-cleaning is not recommended. ■

FLEECE

A TOUCH OF CLASS

The fleece and flannel fabrics today are so diverse and oh so wonderful to work with that you'll really enjoy making projects for every occasion, every room and every age group.

Split-Diamonds Pullover

By Carol Zentgraf

Suede and fleece pair beautifully for construction ease and great design.

Project Specifications
Skill Level: Beginner
Pullover Size: Any size

Materials
- Commercial pullover pattern with yoke designed for fleece, such as Kwik Sew pattern #3001
- Fleece fabric in two colors as suggested on pattern
- Scraps of suede for trim in colors to match fleece
- Self-adhesive, double-sided basting tape
- Teflon sewing machine foot
- Tracing paper
- Basic sewing supplies and tools

Instructions
Step 1. Follow the pattern guide to cut the pieces from fleece.

Step 2. Follow the pattern instructions to sew the yoke front and lower front pieces together. Repeat for yoke back and lower back. Sew the front to the back at the shoulders. Add the collar and sew the tops of the sleeves in place. Do not sew the side or underarm seams.

Step 3. Trace the half-diamond shape onto tracing paper and cut out. Use the pattern to cut three half-diamond shapes from each suede color.

Step 4. Open the garment and place it on a flat work surface, right side up. Refer to the photo to evenly place the diamond halves along the front yoke seam line, slightly overlapping the edges at the seam line. Use self-adhesive, double-sided basting tape to secure the edges of the suede pieces in place.

Step 5. Topstitch close to the edges of each suede trim piece. Topstitch the overlapping edges together at the seam line.

Step 6. Follow pattern instructions to complete pullover. ■

Half-Diamond Pattern

Royal Diamond Pintucks Jacket

By Nancy Fiedler

Use a twin needle and beading foot to add interesting texture to this fleece jacket.

Project Specifications

Skill Level: Beginner
Jacket Size: Any size

Materials

- Commercial jacket pattern such as McCall's #2298
- Fleece yardage as suggested by pattern, plus 1/4 yard to allow shrinkage from pintucks
- 5 (7/8-inch) contrasting buttons
- 2 spools variegated quilting thread in color to contrast with fleece
- 1 cone Woolly Nylon in color to match fleece
- All-purpose thread to match fleece
- Stretch twin needle 4.0/75
- Stretch needle 11/75
- 4mm beading foot for sewing machine
- Tailor's chalk
- 24-inch quilter's ruler with 45-degree angle markings
- Basic sewing supplies and tools

Instructions

Step 1. Wind the bobbin with Woolly Nylon. Insert the twin needle and thread with variegated quilting thread. Attach the 4mm beading foot and set the machine for saddle stitch as shown in **Fig.1**.

Fig. 1 Saddle Stitch

Step 2. Place fleece on work surface, single layer, right side up. With quilter's ruler and tailor's chalk, draw a line at a 45-degree angle to the selvage across the width of the fabric. Place the fabric under the presser foot, centering the line under the twin needle. Sew the first pintuck.

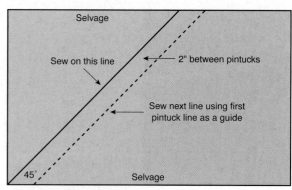

Fig. 2 Stitch pintucks as shown.

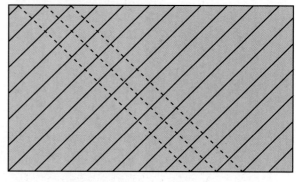

Fig. 3 Stitch pintucks in opposite direction.

Step 3. Attach the seam/quilting guide to the sewing machine and set it 2 inches from the center needle position. Place the fabric under the presser foot, lining up the first pintuck with the seam guide. Sew the next pintuck as shown in **Fig. 2**, using the guide to keep the foot and fabric in position. Repeat this process across the entire piece of fabric.

Step 4. Use the tailor's chalk and quilter's ruler to draw lines in the opposite direction from the first pintucks and sew as shown in **Fig. 3**.

Step 5. Follow the pattern directions to cut out and construct the jacket.

Step 6. For added interest, use variegated quilting thread to make the buttonholes and to finish the facings and hems. ■

Classy Beaded Top
By Lori Blankenship

Soft, warm and cozy can also be chic and stylish!

Project Specifications
Skill Level: Beginner
Top Size: Any size

Materials
- Commercial pattern for no-collar shirt or light jacket, such as Simplicity #5970
- Patterned flannel as required by pattern
- 3 x 30-inch strip of coordinating flannel for inset strip
- 3 x 30-inch strip of contrasting flannel for embellishment strip plus 18 x 18-inch square for bias strips
- $7^{1}/_{4}$ x $8^{1}/_{4}$-inch floral print flannel rectangle for pocket
- $5^{1}/_{2}$ x $8^{1}/_{4}$-inch striped flannel rectangle for pocket
- $4^{3}/_{4}$ x $8^{1}/_{2}$-inch contrasting flannel rectangle for pocket
- 2 yards narrow cotton cord for piping
- 6 oval glass beads, approximately $3/_{8}$ inch by $1/_{2}$ inch to match embellishment strip
- Buttons as suggested by pattern
- All-purpose threads to match fabrics
- Basic sewing supplies and tools

Instructions
Step 1. Cut pattern pieces as directed, transfer markings and stitch darts.

Step 2. On right front, measure 4 inches over from center front and draw a line from shoulder to hem. From that line measure over 1 inch and draw another line shoulder to hem. Cut on the marked lines to remove a section of fabric. Set aside.

Step 3. Turn under long edges of 3 x 30-inch strip of contrasting embellishment flannel $1/_{4}$ inch; press. Turn edges under again $1/_{4}$ inch, press and stitch.

Step 4. Center embellishment strip on 3 x 30-inch inset strip, aligning short edges and with right sides up. Stitch $1/_{4}$ inch from top short edge to hold in place.

Step 5. Place strips on work surface. Measure and mark $5/_{8}$-inch seam allowance across top of both fabrics. On embellishment strip only, mark six sections measuring 5 inches each. Mark the $5/_{8}$-inch seam allowance across the bottom of both fabrics.

Step 6. Fold the embellishment strip back. Begin to mark the inset from the seam allowance

dividing strip into six sections measuring 4⅝ inches each. Fold the embellishment strip back in place.

Step 7. Match marks on embellishment strip to marks on inset strip, pinning in place. Stitch on marked lines. Pinch the center of each section of the embellishment strip, hand-stitch the pinch and secure with one oval glass bead.

Step 8. Pin and stitch the embellished inset strip between the center front sides using a

½-inch seam allowance. Do not catch embellishment strip in seam.

Step 9. Stitch fronts to back at shoulder seams.

Step 10. From 18-inch contrasting flannel square, cut 1½-inch-wide bias strips and sew enough together to make 2 yards of binding.

Step 11. To make piping, place cotton cord down wrong side of center of binding. Fold long edges together, wrong sides facing, and stitch as close to cord as possible with zipper foot.

Step 12. Pin piping to front right side, matching the cut edges and beginning at the bottom. Stitch in place with zipper foot. Repeat on other side. Pin piping around neck edge and stitch in place.

Step 13. Follow pattern directions for attaching the front bands and facings.

Step 14. Add buttons and buttonholes to front band.

Step 15. Add sleeves as per pattern directions, but hem by machine.

Step 16. Turn one long upper edge of the 7¼ x 8¼-inch floral print pocket to the inside ¼ inch; press. Turn the upper edge to the outside 1¾ inches. Stitch around the cut edges, beginning and ending at the folded edge, using ¼-inch seam allowance. Turn the upper edge of pocket right side out. Turn in remaining edges of pocket using stitching line as a guide. Press in place. Repeat for two other pockets.

Step 17. Referring to photo, place pockets on left front. Begin stitching on lowest contrasting layer. Overlap the striped pocket and stitch. Finish with the outer floral pocket on top.

Step 18. Follow pattern instructions for hem, but hem by machine. ■

Out 'n' About Jacket   By Carol Zentgraf

Transform the collars and pockets of any fleece jacket with a sculptured grid pattern.

Project Specifications
Skill Level: Beginner
Jacket Size: Any size

Materials
- Commercial jacket pattern for fleece, such as Simplicity pattern # 3299
- Fleece in yardage indicated on pattern
- $1/4$ yard fusible tear-away stabilizer
- $1/4$ yard water-soluble stabilizer
- Clear acrylic quilter's ruler
- Rayon machine-embroidery thread to match fleece
- All-purpose thread to match fleece
- Buttons and notions as indicated on pattern
- Seam sealant
- Basic sewing supplies and tools

Instructions
Step 1. Follow the pattern guide sheet to cut the pieces from fleece.

Step 2. Fuse tear-away stabilizer to the wrong side of each pocket piece and the upper collar piece. Trim stabilizer even with fleece edges.

Step 3. Mark a grid design on the stabilizer side of each piece by drawing a line through the vertical center. Use this line as a guide to mark lines spaced 1 inch apart across the piece. Repeat to mark horizontal lines.

Step 4. Use rayon machine-embroidery thread in the needle and bobbin and stitch along marked lines to the edges, backstitching at the ends of each line.

Step 5. Apply seam sealant to the ends. Tear away the stabilizer, leaving a 1-inch strip around the outer edges of the pockets.

Step 6. Turn the upper edge of each pocket under $1/2$ inch and topstitch $1/4$ inch from the edge. Pin the pockets to the jacket fronts and topstitch the side and lower edges in place. Remove any stabilizer that shows.

Step 7. Follow pattern instructions to complete the jacket. Stitch three rows of topstitching, spaced $1/2$ inch apart, around each sleeve hem.

Step 8. Use water-soluble stabilizer on each side of the fleece when making buttonholes. ■

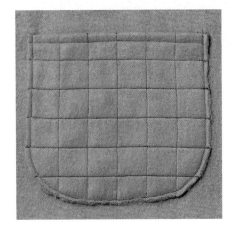

Border Print Pullovers & Hat

By Carol Zentgraf

Expand your creative options when you use fleece with border prints.

Project Specifications
Skill Level: Beginner
Pullover & Hat Sizes: Any size

Materials
- Commercial pullover and hat patterns for fleece, such as Kwik Sew #2817
- Fleece fabrics in yardages outlined below
- All-purpose threads to match fleece
- Basic sewing supplies and tools

Instructions

YARDAGE FOR BORDER PRINTS

Step 1. Place the pattern straight-of-grain markings on the crosswise grain of the fabric instead of the usual lengthwise grain.

Step 2. To calculate yardage needed for fleece with a single border (printed on one edge only), measure the total width of the front, back, sleeve and other pattern pieces to be placed on the border, adding $1/4$-inch seam allowances to each piece. Small pieces, such as collars, facings, pockets or cuffs can be positioned as desired on the border or in the center unprinted area.

Step 3. To calculate the yardage needed for fleece with a double border, measure the total width of the front, back and facing pieces only, adding $1/4$-inch seam allowances to each piece. The sleeves and other pieces will be cut on the opposite edge of the fabric.

Step 4. If there is a definite repeat to the design or you want to match it to the seam lines, allow for an extra repeat when calculating the yardage.

Step 5. To calculate the yardage for either type of border print for a hat, measure the longest piece to be placed along the border, usually the brim.

PATTERN LAYOUT

Border at Garment Lower Edge

Step 1. For a single border fabric, place the front, back, facing and sleeve pieces with the hem edges toward the selvage. Be sure all pieces are an equal distance from the edge to ensure design continuity.

Step 2. For a double border print fabric, place the front, back and facing pieces on one edge with the hem edges evenly spaced from the selvage. Place the sleeves and any other pieces, such as collars or pockets, along the opposite edge.

Step 3. To lay out hat pattern pieces on either type of print, place the brim pieces parallel to the selvage edges. If the brim turns up and the print is directional, be sure to position the under brim piece so the design will be right side up when the brim is flipped up.

Border at Garment Upper Edge

Step 1. Follow the instructions above, reversing the direction of the pattern pieces. Be sure that the front and back shoulder seams are the same distance from the edge.

CONSTRUCTION

Step 1. Follow the layout instructions above to cut the pattern pieces from the fleece.

Step 2. Follow the pattern instructions to complete the pullovers and hat. ■

Gold Braid Evening Vest

By Marian Shenk

Gold braid and embellishments make this simple black vest a very dressy garment.

Project Specifications
Skill Level: Beginner
Vest Size: Any size

Materials
- Commercial vest pattern such as Simplicity pattern #7320
- $3/4$ yard black micro-fleece
- $3/4$ yard black lining fabric
- 10 yards $1/4$-inch-wide gold metallic braid
- 11 ($3/4$-inch) gold metallic flowers
- 11 ($1/4$-inch) pearl beads
- Black all-purpose thread
- Gold metallic thread
- Lightweight cardboard $6^{1}/_{2}$ inches by 8 inches
- Craft knife
- White chalk marker
- Basic sewing supplies and tools

Instructions
Step 1. Using view C of vest pattern, cut out two fronts and one back. Sew fronts to back and press seams open.

Step 2. Trace braid design on lightweight cardboard. With craft knife, create a stencil by cutting out shaded areas of design. Trace in connecting sections on vest fronts and back with white chalk marker as shown in **Fig. 1**.

Step 3. In one continuous line, pin $1/4$-inch-wide gold metallic braid on marked lines, overlapping braid at center of the three petals. With gold metallic thread, stitch in place; press.

Step 4. Place vest on lining fabric, right sides facing. Pin around outside edges. Cut out lining to match vest. There will be no side seams in lining.

Step 5. Starting at the neckline edge of shoulder, sew down front, across back and up to other shoulder. Sew around the armholes and across the back neckline.

Step 6. Clip seams on curves and turn right side out, pulling the vest through one of the shoulder openings; press.

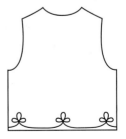

Fig. 1 In one continuous line, trace braid design on vest fronts and back as shown, overlapping at the center of the 3 petals.

Step 7. Pin shoulder seams together, right sides facing, and stitch. Open up and hand-stitch the lining closed on the inside.

Step 8. Hand-sew the gold metallic flowers and pearl beads to the center of each design as shown in photo. ■

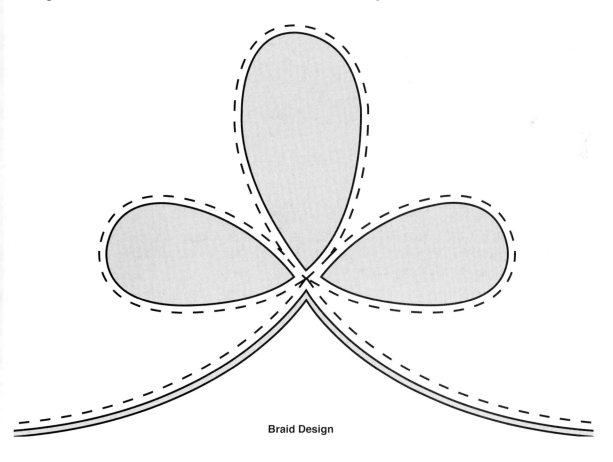

Braid Design

Snips & Tucks Vest By Lori Blankenship

Fleece is a pleasure and a joy when it comes to finishing edges—you don't need to!

Project Specifications
Skill Level: Beginner
Vest Size: Any size

Materials
- Commercial unlined zippered vest pattern, such as Simplicity #9820
- Fleece in yardage required by pattern
- $1/3$ yard contrasting fleece for pockets and trim
- 22-inch separating zipper to match vest
- All-purpose threads to match fabrics
- 4 ($1/4$-inch) glass beads to match contrasting fleece
- Rotary cutter and mat
- Basic sewing supplies and tools

Instructions
Step 1. Measure and mark $8^{1}/_{2}$ inches down from the center of the shoulder of vest front pattern. Fold the pattern at the mark from arm opening to center front. Cut on the fold lines. Add $1/2$-inch extension to each piece for seam allowance. These pieces will be the upper and lower vest fronts.

Step 2. From vest fleece and contrasting fleece, cut two upper front pieces each. The contrasting pieces will be lining. From vest fleece, cut two lower vest fronts.

Step 3. From vest fleece, cut one vest back and two pocket trim pieces $6^{1}/_{2}$ x $1^{1}/_{2}$ inches. From contrasting fleece, cut one back facing, two patch pockets $6^{1}/_{2}$ x 9 inches and two vest trim strips $1^{1}/_{2}$ x 10 inches.

Step 4. Fold $1^{1}/_{2}$ x 10-inch vest trim strips in half to measure $3/4$ x 10 inches. Pin to lower edges of upper vest fronts, matching cut edges and tapering at seam lines to lessen bulk. Stitch in place using $1/2$-inch seam allowances. Match and pin the lower vest fronts to the upper vest fronts, right sides facing, with trim sandwiched between. Stitch in place using previous stitching line as a guide.

Step 5. Follow pattern instructions for inserting zipper.

Step 6. Stitch vest fronts to back at shoulder seams.

Step 7. Turn lower edge of back neck facing and upper vest lining under $1/4$ inch; stitch. Stitch back neck facing to upper vest lining at shoulder seams.

Step 8. With right sides facing, pin facing and lining to vest, matching shoulder seams, upper vest front and arm opening. Stitch along the armhole opening, front and neck edges using $5/8$-inch seam allowance. Trim seams and turn vest right side out. Finger-press the seam lines.

Step 9. Stitch vest fronts to back at side

seams. Clip the corners of the underarm seam allowance.

Step 10. Turn the cut edges of the armhole openings under ¹/₄ inch. Turn over another ¹/₄ inch to follow seamed area of upper vest front. Stitch around the entire armhole opening.

Step 11. Anchor the upper vest lining to vest at shoulder seams and lower edge of upper vest. Trim seams when necessary to reduce bulk.

Step 12. Turn the top edge of each pocket down 1¹/₄ inches. Topstitch 1 inch from the top edge. Use the pocket template to mark cutting lines. Cut on marked lines. Weave 6¹/₂ x 1¹/₂-inch vest trim strip through cuts as shown in photo. Repeat for two pockets.

Step 13. Pinch up the exposed pocket sections and stitch. Sew a glass bead to each area.

Step 14. Center the pockets on the front vest

pieces between the side seams and zipper top-stitching. Turn the pocket sides under ¹/₂ inch and pin in place. Stitch around pockets, anchoring the top of each pocket seam with a bar tack.

Step 15. Turn the bottom edge of the vest under 1 inch and topstitch in place.

Step 16. Place the upper vest cutting template perpendicular to upper/lower right vest trim strip and approximately 2 inches from zipper topstitching. Pin in place and mark cutting lines. Use rotary cutter to cut through both layers of fleece on upper vest cutting lines. Use sharp scissors to even up each slit.

Step 17. Reverse template on other vest front, mark and cut.

Step 18. Starting at the top slit, pull lining through to the front and fold over the top of the matching vest strip as shown in photo. Pin in place and continue on all strips.

SNIPS & TUCKS VEST

Stitching Line

Pocket Cutting Template

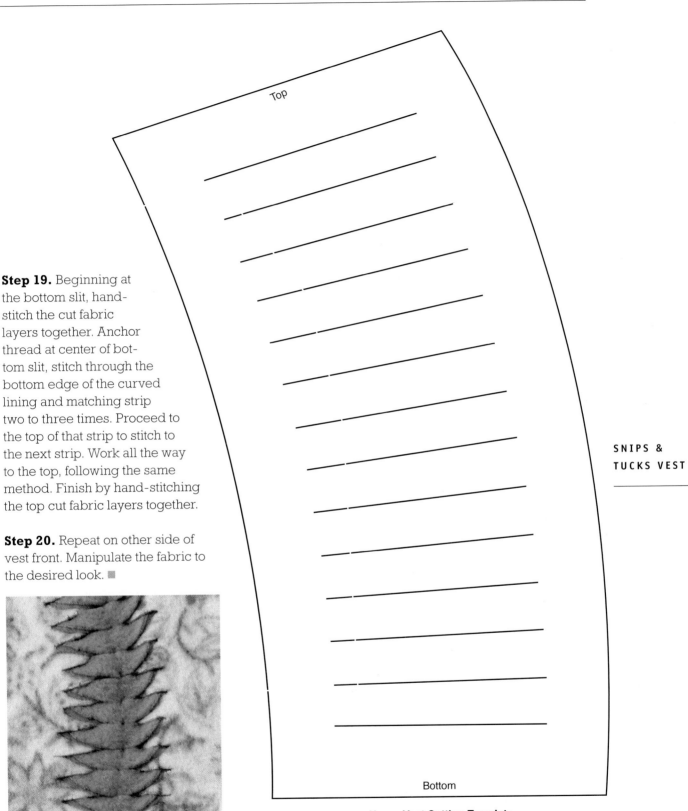

Step 19. Beginning at the bottom slit, hand-stitch the cut fabric layers together. Anchor thread at center of bottom slit, stitch through the bottom edge of the curved lining and matching strip two to three times. Proceed to the top of that strip to stitch to the next strip. Work all the way to the top, following the same method. Finish by hand-stitching the top cut fabric layers together.

Step 20. Repeat on other side of vest front. Manipulate the fabric to the desired look. ▧

Top

Bottom

Upper Vest Cutting Template

Sculpted Fleece Pajamas

By Carol Zentgraf

Bring on the winter weather! The designer touches applied to this cozy set will have you ready and waiting.

Project Specifications
Skill Level: Beginner
Pajama Size: Any size

Materials
- Commercial pajama pattern for fleece, such as Kwik Sew pattern #2907
- Fleece in yardage suggested on pattern
- 1 yard fusible tear-away stabilizer
- Scraps of water-soluble stabilizer

- Clear acrylic quilter's ruler with 45-degree angles and inch marks
- Rayon machine-embroidery thread that contrasts with fleece
- All-purpose thread to match fleece
- Buttons and elastic as suggested on pattern
- Seam sealant
- Rotary cutter with pinking blade
- Basic sewing supplies and tools

Instructions
Step 1. Follow pattern guide sheet to cut pajama pattern pieces from fleece.

Step 2. Construct pajama pants as instructed on pattern.

Step 3. Fuse tear-away stabilizer to wrong side of each pajama top front piece. Trim the stabilizer even with the fleece edges.

Step 4. Mark the diamond design on the stabilizer side of each front piece by aligning the 45-degree-angle mark on the ruler with the lower edge of the piece. Draw a diagonal line across the piece. Use this line as a guide to mark diagonal lines spaced 2 inches apart across the entire piece. Repeat to mark diagonal lines in the opposite direction to create diamonds.

Step 5. Use rayon machine-embroidery thread

in the machine needle and bobbin. Stitch along marked lines to ¹/₄ inch from edges, backstitching at the ends of each line. Apply seam sealant to the ends. Do not tear away the stabilizer.

Step 6. Follow the pattern directions to complete the pajama top. Use the rotary cutter with pinking blade to trim the collar, front and lower edges. Topstitch ¹/₄ inch from the edges.

Step 7. Follow the pattern directions to mark the buttonholes, using a piece of water-soluble stabilizer on top of each buttonhole. Stitch and cut the buttonholes. Remove the stabilizer from the buttonholes and the wrong side of the fronts.

Step 8. Sew on buttons. ■

SCULPTED
FLEECE
PAJAMAS

Roll-Up Jewelry Pouch

By Mary Ayres

Protect your fine jewelry in this soft flannel bag—
perfect for travel!

Project Specifications

Skill Level: Beginner
Jewelry Pouch Size: Approximately
    6 x 11 inches (open)

Materials

- Multicolor flannel print 6$\frac{1}{2}$ x 11$\frac{1}{2}$ inches for outside of bag
- $\frac{1}{4}$ yard coordinating mottled print flannel for bag lining and pockets
- 2 yards coordinating piping
- 28-inch piece of coordinating 1-inch-wide satin ribbon
- Basic sewing supplies and tools

Instructions

Step 1. From coordinating mottled print flannel, cut 10 rectangles 3 x 6$\frac{1}{2}$ inches for pockets.

Step 2. On five of the rectangles, sew piping to

right side of fabric across one long side ¼ inch from the edge.

Step 3. Place one each of the five remaining rectangles on each of the piped rectangles, right sides facing. Stitch together along the previous piping stitching.

Step 4. On four of the piping rectangles, stitch across opposite long sides ¼ inch from the edge, forming tubes. The rectangle that has stitching only on piped edge is for the bottom pocket.

Step 5. Turn rectangles with right sides facing out.

Step 6. From coordinating mottled print flannel, cut a rectangle 6½ x 11½ inches for bag lining. Pin one pocket tube horizontally to the right side of the lining rectangle. The piping edge should be 2¾ inches down from the top edge with side edges aligned. Stitch the pocket to the lining along sides and bottom, close to edge.

Step 7. Pin another pocket tube horizontally to the lining rectangle. The piping edge should be 1½ inches down from the top edge of the first pocket with sides aligned with the lining rectangle. Stitch pocket to large rectangle along the sides and bottom close to edge.

Step 8. Repeat Step 7 two more times.

Step 9. Pin remaining pocket, which is not a tube, to the right side of the lining rectangle. Align bottom and side edges. Stitch pocket to lining along sides and bottom close to the edge.

Step 10. Sew piping around right side of lining rectangle, ¼ inch from the edge, beginning and ending at a corner.

Step 11. Place multicolor flannel print rectangle on lining rectangle, right sides facing. Sew

ROLL-UP
JEWELRY
POUCH

along previous piping stitching, leaving a 3-inch opening along one side for turning.

Step 12. Trim corners and turn bag right side out. Close opening with hand stitches.

Step 13. Fold 28-inch piece of 1-inch-wide satin ribbon in half. Stitch fold to center bottom of bag on the outside.

Step 14. Place jewelry in bag pockets and roll bag up from top to bottom. Wrap ribbon around rolled up bag and tie in a bow. Trim ribbon ends even in a V shape. ∎

Red Tulip Pillow By June Fiechter

The depth of flannel colors used in this pillow create a rich, stained glass design.

Project Specifications
Skill Level: Beginner
Pillow Size: 16 x 16 inches

Materials
- 1 square cream flannel 12 x 12 inches
- 1 rectangle red flannel 11 x 6½ inches
- 2 squares green flannel 17 x 17 inches and

- 1 square 2 x 2 inches
- 2 yards ¼-inch-wide fusible black bias
- 16 x 16-inch pillow form
- Black and cream all-purpose thread
- ¼ yard fusible web
- Fabric glue
- 1 x 1-inch square of hook-and-loop tape
- Basic sewing supplies and tools

Instructions
Step 1. Center one strip of ¼-inch-wide fusible black bias on one 17 x 17-inch green flannel square. Following manufacturer's instructions, fuse in place. With black thread, stitch very close to both edges of bias. This will be the pillow front.

Step 2. Trace stained glass shapes on paper side of fusible web as instructed on patterns. Cut out, leaving roughly ¼-inch margin around shapes. Fuse to selected fabrics following manufacturer's instructions. Cut out shapes on traced lines.

Step 3. Cut 12 x 12-inch cream flannel square in half diagonally. Place triangle on work surface.

Step 4. Referring to photo, place fused pieces on triangle point, overlapping as necessary. Leave 1/4-inch seam allowance at outer edges of triangle. Fuse, following manufacturer's instructions.

Step 5. Place fusible black bias over all cut edges, except outer triangle edges; fuse. With black thread, stitch very close to both edges of bias.

Step 6. Place second cream flannel triangle over fused piece, right sides facing. Stitch along sides, leaving long edge open. Turn right side out and press.

Step 7. Place and fuse black bias over remaining edges of fused triangle.

Step 8. Turn under 1/4 inch and stitch the top edge of pillow front made in Step 1.

Step 9. Right sides facing, stitch open edge of cream triangle to remaining 17 x 17-inch green flannel square.

Step 10. Place green flannel squares together, right sides facing. Stitch around three sides, leaving top open.

Step 11. Position hook-and-loop squares on back side of cream triangle and right side of pillow front. Glue in place with fabric glue.

Step 12. Insert pillow form and fasten hook-and-loop squares. ▪

RED TULIP
PILLOW

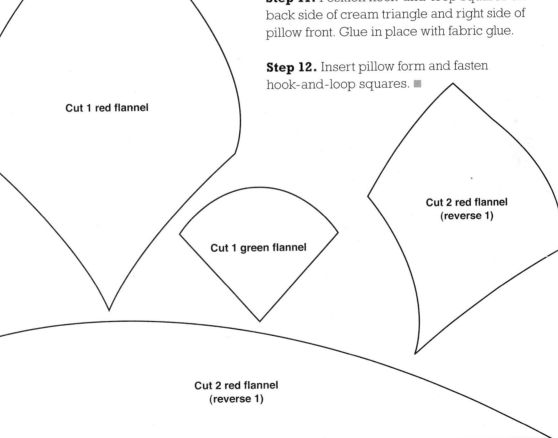

Cut 1 red flannel

Cut 1 green flannel

Cut 2 red flannel
(reverse 1)

Cut 2 red flannel
(reverse 1)

Reversible Drawstring Bag

By Lori Blankenship

Sturdy, but pretty—this bag will hold loads and loads!

Project Specifications
Skill Level: Beginner
Bag Size: Approximately 19 x 16 x 4½ inches

Materials
- ⅝ yard floral fleece for bag
- ⅝ yard contrasting fleece for lining
- All-purpose threads to match fabrics
- 2 yards of ³⁄₁₆-inch coordinating decorator cord
- 2 (¾-inch) glass beads with large holes

- Rotary-cutting tools
- Chalk marker
- Craft glue
- Basic sewing supplies and tools

Instructions
Step 1. Cut two squares each from both fleece fabrics 20 x 20 inches for bag and lining. From each fleece fabric, cut one rectangle each 20 x 9 inches for pockets. From each fleece fabric, cut one bag bottom each using pattern provided.

Step 2. Turn one long edge of each pocket piece under ¼ inch and topstitch in place.

Step 3. Pin one pocket to one matching bag section, aligning bottom and side edges. To form pocket sections, measure in 6½ inches from each side and stitch from bottom to top of pocket through both layers.

Step 4. Place two bag sections together, right sides facing, and sew side seams. Match side seams to marks on bag bottom; pin. Stitch in place. Trim and clip curves.

Step 5. Place bag on flat surface. Measure down 4½ inches from top and mark with chalk around entire bag. Mark on bag only. Use rotary cutter and cut 4-inch fringe every ½ inch to chalk line.

Step 6. Repeat Steps 3–5 to make bag lining.

Step 7. Insert lining bag in outer bag, wrong sides together. Smooth out the fringe and stitch on the chalk line to form the bottom of the casing.

Step 8. Thread one glass bead on each end of decorator cord. Secure with craft glue. Tie ends in a loose knot. Coil cord to form a double circle.

Step 9. Separate the fringe by color. Place the cord between the layers of separated fringe. Tie knots, using one strand from each layer, over the cord to form the top of the casing. Pull on ends of cord to draw bag closed. ■

**REVERSIBLE
DRAWSTRING
BAG**

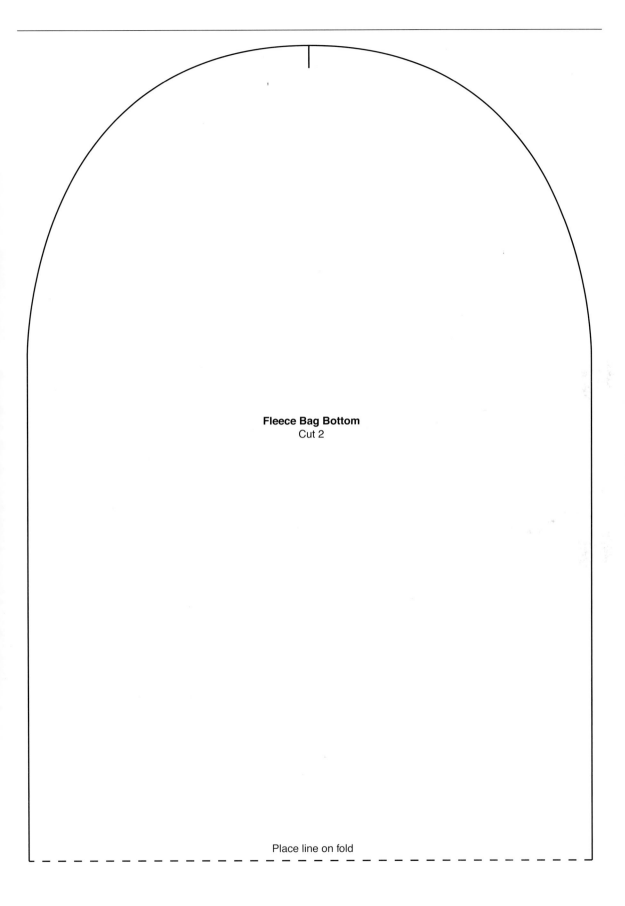

Fleece Bag Bottom
Cut 2

REVERSIBLE
DRAWSTRING
BAG

Place line on fold

Soft Sweet Shirt By June Fiechter

Soft, restful, white and comfortable!

Project Specifications
Skill Level: Beginner
Shirt Size: Any size

Materials
- Commercial shirt pattern such as New Look pattern #6976
- $1^3/_8$ yards white flannel
- $1^1/_2$ yards sheer white cotton fabric
- 1 yard of $^1/_8$ inch white cotton cord
- Variety of clear glass beads
- 2 packages $^1/_2$-inch-wide white single-fold bias tape
- White 6-strand embroidery floss
- Embroidery needle
- White all-purpose thread
- $^2/_3$ yard of $^1/_4$-inch white elastic
- 1 safety pin
- Basic sewing supplies and tools

Instructions
Step 1. Make shirt, View A, as directed in pattern instructions. Cut the body from white flannel and sleeves from sheer white cotton. Use the $^1/_8$-inch-wide cotton cord at neckline instead of making a tie.

Step 2. With white single-fold bias tape, cover the seam allowance where sleeves attach to the body. Sew tape to the body.

Step 3. Cut $2^1/_2$ inches from the ends of the sleeves and the bottom of the body.

Step 4. From sheer white cotton fabric, cut two 3-inch-wide bias strips the length of the body front and back lower edges and two 3-inch-wide bias strips the length of the ends of each sleeve. This will be determined by your pattern size.

Step 5. If your sewing machine has an attachment to roll hems, roll one edge of each bias strip. If not, turn under the narrowest hem possible (about $^3/_{16}$ inch) and stitch.

Step 6. Stitch raw edges of strips to bottom of body and ends of sleeves.

Embroidery Line Pattern

Fig. 1 Trace embroidery line pattern along right side of neckline. Reverse on left side.

Step 7. Use 1/2-inch-wide bias tape to enclose seam allowance at lower body edge as in sleeves, Step 2.

Step 8. With 1/2-inch-wide bias tape, create a casing over the seam at lower edge of sleeves.

Step 9. Measure two lengths of elastic to fit comfortably around arms (3/4-length sleeves). Attach safety pin to one end of elastic and thread through casing. Secure ends of elastic and close opening in casing. Repeat for second sleeve.

Step 10. Lightly trace embroidery line pattern along right side of neckline as shown in **Fig. 1**. Reverse the pattern on the left side of neckline. With 6 strands of white embroidery floss, work stem stitch along traced line, attaching a variety of clear glass beads randomly along the line.

Step 11. Sew a variety of clear glass beads randomly across the front of the top. ■

White on White Evening Bag

By June Fiechter

The glitter of thread and crystals makes a lovely contrast in texture with soft, white flannel.

Project Specifications
Skill Level: Beginner
Purse Size: Approximately $5^1/_2$ x 6 x $1^1/_2$ inches

Materials
- 5 x 5-inch square of white flannel
- 4 pieces of white flannel 7 x 8 inches
- 2 strips of white flannel 2 x $16^1/_4$ inches
- 5 x 5-inch square of fusible web
- 3 ($3/_{16}$-inch) crystals
- $5^1/_2$-inch-wide gold purse clasp
- 1 yard gold purse chain
- White metallic thread
- All-purpose white thread
- Fabric glue
- Basic sewing supplies and tools

Instructions
Step 1. Trace petals on paper side of 5 x 5-inch fusible web square as instructed on pattern, leaving approximately $1/_4$-inch margin around each shape.

Step 2. Bond fusible web to 5 x 5-inch white flannel square, following manufacturer's instructions. Cut out petals on traced lines.

Step 3. Trace and cut four bag shapes from white flannel.

Step 4. Select one bag shape as front. Trace vines and position petals as shown on pattern; fuse.

Step 5. With white metallic thread, sew a running stitch around the inside of each petal. Sew traced vine lines with running stitch.

Step 6. Glue crystals in the center of each blossom.

Step 7. Sew one 2 x $16^1/_4$-inch flannel strip around the bag front as shown in **Fig. 1**. Sew remaining side of strip to another bag shape for bag back. This will be the bag body. Repeat with remaining strip and bag pieces for bag lining.

Fig. 1 Sew strip around bag front as shown.

Step 8. Place bag lining inside bag body, wrong sides facing. Turn top edges in and sew to secure.

Step 9. Tuck top edge of bag inside purse clasp and stitch in place. Tack in place at bag sides.

Step 10. Attach gold purse chain to purse clasp. ∎

WHITE ON
WHITE
EVENING
BAG

Petal
Cut 19 white flannel

Bag Pattern
Cut 4 white flannel

SOFT
HOLIDAY
ACCENTS

The fleece and flannel of today is so soft. It's perfect for decorating your home for the holiday, adding just the right tough.

Holiday Spirit Vest By Carol Zentgraf

Two vests in one—with just a quick change of the pockets you can vary the holiday look.

Project Specifications
Skill Level: Beginner
Vest Size: Any size

Materials
- Commercial vest pattern designed for fleece
- $1/6$ yard red fleece
- Red fleece in yardage recommended on pattern
- 2 packages (3 yards each) black fleece double-fold binding
- Green, red, white, gold and pink felt scraps
- 4 silver clasp closures
- 4 ($1/2$-inch) silver buttons
- $1/4$ yard black fusible interfacing
- $3/4$ yard $3/4$-inch-wide black hook-and-loop tape
- Scraps of water-soluble stabilizer
- Red 6-strand embroidery floss
- Red and black all-purpose thread
- Tapestry needle
- Fabric glue
- Basic sewing supplies and tools

Instructions
Step 1. Follow pattern instructions to make vest, using overlapping seams and a center-front closure. Bind the edges and armholes with black fleece binding.

Step 2. Evenly space and sew silver clasp closures to center front edges.

Step 3. Cut four 5 x 5$1/2$-inch rectangles each from black fleece and black fusible interfacing for pockets. Following manufacturer's instructions, fuse interfacing to wrong sides of fleece pocket pieces.

Step 4. On each pocket piece mark two $1/2$-inch-long buttonholes $1/2$ inch from the side edges and $1/4$ inch from the upper edge as shown in **Fig. 1**. Stitch the buttonholes, using water-soluble stabilizer on top of the fleece. Remove the stabilizer and cut the buttonholes open.

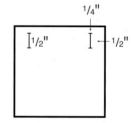

Fig. 1 Make buttonholes as shown.

Step 5. Thread tapestry needle with 6 strands of red embroidery floss. Stitch a running stitch around the edges of each pocket, making an X in each lower corner. The stitches should be approximately $5/8$ inch in length.

Step 6. Trace and cut Christmas tree, star and circle shapes as directed on patterns. Referring

Continued on page 82

Jolly Holly Pillows By Carol Zentgraf

Fleece is a holiday helper! It's quick and easy and so pleasant to work with.

Project Specifications
Skill Level: Beginner
Holly Sprig Pillow Size: 16 x 16 inches
Holly Wreath Pillow Size: 18 x 18 inches

Materials
- 1 pillow form 16 x 16 inches
- 1 pillow form 18 x 18 inches
- 1 yard green fleece
- 1¹/₂ yards red fleece
- 2 (³/₄-inch) red buttons with shanks
- 6 (¹/₂-inch) red buttons with shanks
- 2 yards 2¹/₂-inch-wide sheer wire-edged gold ribbon
- 2 yards (1-inch) cotton cord for holly sprig pillow welting
- Rotary cutter with regular and zigzag blades
- Cutting mat and clear quilter's ruler
- White air-soluble marker
- Self-adhesive, double-sided basting tape
- Red 6-strand embroidery floss
- All-purpose threads to match fabrics
- Basic sewing supplies and tools

Instructions

HOLLY SPRIG PILLOW

Step 1. From red fleece, cut two 17 x 17-inch squares for pillow front and back. Trace and cut five holly leaves from green fleece. Trace veins on leaves with white air-soluble marker.

Step 2. From green fleece, cut enough 3-inch-wide strips to make a total of 66 inches.

Step 3. Referring to the photo, position holly leaves on one red 17 x 17-inch square. Use self-adhesive, double-sided basting tape to secure the center of each leaf.

Step 4. Referring to the photo for placement, draw the stems and veins with white air-soluble marker. With a 4.0 machine stitch, sew along the stem and vein lines with green thread.

HOLLY
JOLLY
PILLOWS

Step 5. To make welting, wrap the 3-inch by 66-inch green strip around the 1-inch cotton cord, overlapping ends as needed. With the long edges of the fleece strip aligned, use zipper foot and baste $1/8$ inch from the cord. Trim the fleece lip to $1/2$ inch.

Step 6. Align the lip edge with the appliquéd pillow panel edge. Sew in place, close to the cord. To join the cord ends, cut the ends to butt together and trim the fleece strip to a 1-inch overlap.

Step 7. Referring to the photo for placement, sew the $3/4$-inch red buttons to the top cluster of holly leaves.

Step 8. Cut a 22-inch length of sheer wire-edged gold ribbon and tie in a bow with streamers. Sew to the other set of holly leaves.

Step 9. Pin the pillow back to the pillow front, right sides facing. Using the welt stitching as a guide, stitch around the perimeter, leaving an opening for turning.

Step 10. Turn right side out. Insert pillow form and close opening with hand stitches.

HOLLY WREATH PILLOW

Step 1. From red fleece, cut two 19-inch squares for pillow front and back.

Step 2. Trace and cut 13 holly leaves from green fleece. Trace veins on leaves with white air-soluble marker.

Step 3. From green fleece, cut 5-inch fringe strips to total 72 inches.

Step 4. Referring to the photo for placement, position the leaves in a wreath shape on one pillow square. Use self-adhesive double-sided basting tape to secure the center of each leaf.

Step 5. With a 4.0 machine stitch, sew along the stem and vein lines with green thread.

Step 6. Using the rotary cutter with zigzag blade, trim the edges of each pillow panel. On the wrong side of the front panel, use basting tape to adhere the edge of the fringe strips to the panel edge, overlapping $1/2$ inch. Turn the panel over and zigzag-stitch $1/4$ inch from the edge.

Step 7. Referring to the photo, sew six $1/2$-inch red buttons to the wreath.

Step 8. Cut a $1^{1}/_{4}$-yard length of sheer wire-edged gold ribbon and tie into a bow with streamers. Tack to the wreath as shown in photo.

Step 9. Pin the pillow front to the pillow back, wrong sides facing. Stitch around perimeter, leaving an opening to insert pillow form. Insert the pillow form and continue stitching to close.

Step 10. Use rotary cutter with regular blade and quilter's ruler to cut fringe strip into $1/2$-inch-wide strips up to the pillow edge.

Step 11. Cut 2-inch lengths of 6-strand embroidery floss. Tie fringe strips together in clusters of three strips each. ■

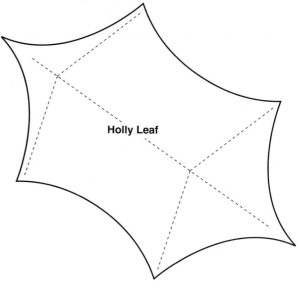

Holly Leaf

JOLLY HOLLY PILLOWS

Festive Christmas Place Mats

By June Fiechter

Choose either of the two appliqué patterns included for a matched set of place mats or mix and match for additional fun.

Project Specifications
Skill Level: Beginner
Place Mat Size: Approximately 17¹/₂ x 11¹/₂ inches

Materials
Note: *Materials are for one place mat.*
- Scraps of green, white, tan and brown flannel as needed for selected appliqué
- 2 red flannel rectangles 18 x 12 inches
- 1 rectangle thin cotton batting 18 x 12 inches
- All-purpose threads to match fabrics
- 2 (¹/₄-inch) black beads for reindeer eyes, if needed
- Fabric glue
- Basic sewing supplies and tools

Instructions
Step 1. Fold flannel and batting rectangles in quarters and round corners to create ovals as shown in **Fig. 1**.

Step 2. Referring to photo, use patterns to cut appliqué shapes of choice from flannel scraps. Cut the snow for the reindeer place mat free-form; use the place mat oval to cut the lower edge to match and gently round the upper edge as you choose.

Step 3. Baste one red flannel oval to batting oval around outer edge.

Step 4. Referring to photo, position appliqué pieces on flannel side of basted ovals. Remove one appliqué piece at a time and spread fabric glue evenly over the back of the piece. Reposition on flannel oval. Continue until all pieces are glued, including reindeer eyes if used.

Step 5. Allow glue to dry thoroughly. Use decorative machine stitch to secure pieces to fabric/batting oval.

Step 6. Position remaining red flannel oval on top of appliquéd oval. Sew around oval with ¹/₄-inch seam allowance, leaving 5-inch opening for turning.

Step 7. Turn place mat right side out and close opening with hand stitches.

Step 8. Topstitch around oval ¹/₄ inch from edge. ◼

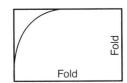

Fig. 1 Fold and round corners to create ovals as shown.

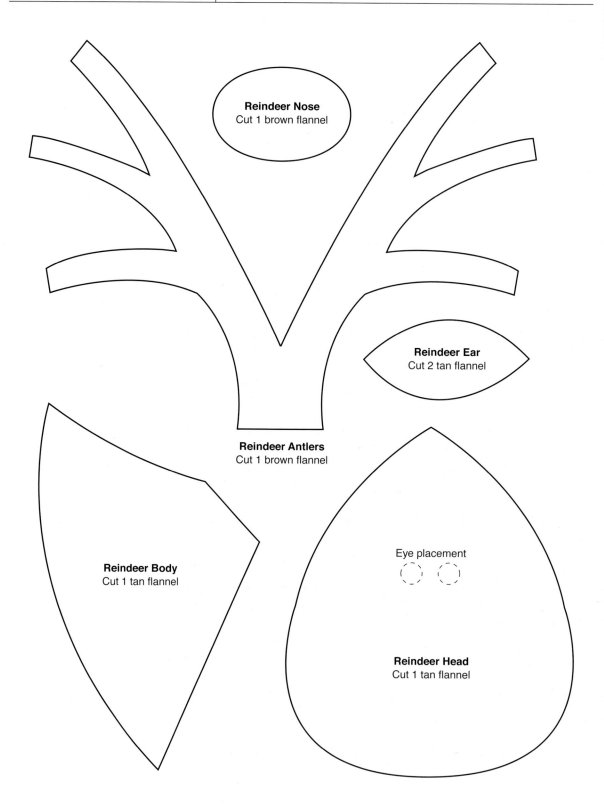

Reindeer Nose
Cut 1 brown flannel

Reindeer Ear
Cut 2 tan flannel

Reindeer Antlers
Cut 1 brown flannel

Reindeer Body
Cut 1 tan flannel

Eye placement

Reindeer Head
Cut 1 tan flannel

Drawings continued on page 82

Holiday Gift Bags By Diana Stunell-Dunsmore

These cute and highly unusual bags are a gift themselves.

Project Specifications

Skill Level: Beginner
Gift Bag Size: Approximately 6$^1/_2$ x 11 inches

Materials

Note: *Materials are for one bag.*

- 2 rectangles chenille fleece 7$^1/_4$ x 10$^1/_4$ inches for bag
- $^1/_8$ yard contrasting single-face fleece
- $^1/_4$ yard white lambskin fleece for animal face
- Scraps of lightweight fusible interfacing
- Scraps of quilt batting
- Small amount of polyester fiberfill
- $^5/_8$ yard $^1/_4$-inch-wide ribbon to match bag, optional for bag closure
- Cosmetic blush
- Craft glue
- All-purpose threads to match fabrics
- White quilting thread for whiskers
- Long needle for whiskers
- Basic sewing supplies and tools

For Bunny Only

- 2$^1/_2$ x 2$^1/_2$-inch square pink lambskin fleece for nose
- 2 x 3-inch scrap of white satin for teeth
- $^3/_4$ yard 1$^1/_2$-inch-wide pink satin ribbon
- 2 ($^1/_2$-inch) round buttons for eyes
- 2 pink silk rosebuds

For Mouse Only

- 2 x 2-inch square of red cotton knit for nose
- $^1/_8$ yard contrasting single-face fleece for scarf
- 5 x 5-inch square of fusible web
- 2 ($^1/_2$-inch) black oval buttons for eyes

BUNNY

Instructions

Step 1. Press under ⁵/₈ inch along one short edge of both chenille bag pieces; stitch. Place both chenille bag pieces right sides together. Sew down one long side, across the bottom and up the other long side with ⁵/₈-inch seam allowance. Trim bottom points, turn right side out and press.

Step 2. Cut bunny ears as instructed on pattern. Fuse interfacing pieces to wrong side of each ear front. Place backs of each ear on interfaced ear fronts, right sides facing. Sew around ears with ¹/₄-inch seam allowance, leaving bottom edges open. Trim seam, clip curves and turn right side out; press.

Step 3. Topstitch each bunny ear at bend as indicated on pattern.

Step 4. Cut bunny faces as instructed on pattern. Mark eye placement on face front. Mark ear placement on wrong side of face front. Sew batting to wrong side of face front.

Step 5. Carefully cut a 2¹/₂-inch vertical slit down the center of the fleece face back.

Step 6. Pin bunny ears to face front, right sides facing. Sew in place.

Step 7. Pin face front to face back, right sides facing. Sew all around face with ¹/₄-inch seam allowance, being careful to keep ears out of the seam. Trim seam, clip curves and turn right side out; press. Close back opening with hand stitches.

Step 8. Cut bunny teeth as instructed on pattern. Fuse interfacing to wrong side of one satin piece. Place teeth right sides together and sew around, leaving top open. Trim seam, clip corners, turn right side out and press. With light gray thread, stitch a line up the center of the teeth to divide.

Step 9. Cut bunny cheeks as instructed on pattern. Using doubled thread, run a gathering stitch around the perimeter of one cheek. Pull the thread up enough to form a cup to fill lightly with polyester fiberfill. The finished cheek should be approximately ³/₄ inch thick and about the size of the solid inner circle indicated on pattern. Knot off the thread. Repeat for second cheek, but do not cut thread after knotting off.

Step 10. Place cheeks side by side on face and secure with pins. Place teeth under cheeks. Secure cheeks with running stitches through the back of the cheeks and top face layer. Catch upper edge of teeth in stitching. When cheeks and teeth are secure, run a few stitches ladder-style between the cheeks to keep them together. A little craft glue may be used to secure the teeth if desired.

Step 11. Cut bunny nose as instructed on pattern. Run a gathering stitch of doubled thread around the perimeter. Stuff with a small amount of polyester fiberfill to the size and shape of the inner line on pattern. Knot off, but do not break thread. Sew nose to face in same manner as cheeks. Sew lower edges of nose to cheeks.

Step 12. Sew on round button eyes.

Step 13. With thread that matches gift bag, stitch bunny face to gift bag, sewing only through the back of face, close to edge.

Step 14. If silk flowers have a stem, tuck behind head and take extra stitches to secure. If there are not stems, glue flowers to bag.

Step 15. Tie 1¹/₂-inch-wide pink satin ribbon in a bow. Tack knot to bag below bunny chin.

Step 16. If you choose to use a ribbon bag

closure, cut $1/4$-inch-wide ribbon in half. Fold one end under $1/4$ inch twice; press. Hand-sew folded ribbon to center of bag front and back.

Step 17. Thread long needle with white quilting thread for whiskers. Refer to **Fig. 1** for stitch placement. Insert needle at A and exit at B, leaving a tail of 2 inches at A. Go in at A and out at C, in at D and out at C. Cut a 2-inch whisker at C.

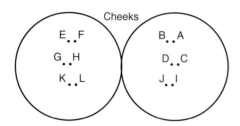

Fig. 1 Stitch whiskers for bunny as shown.

Step 18. Move to the other cheek and take thread in at E, exit at F, leaving a tail of 2 inches at E. Go in again at E, out at G, in at H, out at G. Cut the G whisker 2 inches long.

Step 19. For lower whiskers, take thread in at I, exit at J, leaving a 2-inch tail on the I side. Go in at I and take thread right through to the other cheek and come out at K, in at L and out again at K. Trim this last whisker to 2 inches.

Step 20. Use cosmetic blush and a light hand to carefully apply blush to cheeks and small area of inner ears near the head.

MOUSE

Step 1. Sew chenille bag and construct Mouse ears as in Bunny Steps 1 and 2. Topstitch mouse ears $3/8$ inch from edge on rounded sides.

Step 2. Cut and construct face as in Bunny Steps 4–7, inserting mouse ears instead of bunny ears.

Step 3. Cut mouse nose as instructed on pattern. Run a gathering stitch of doubled thread around the perimeter. Stuff with a small amount of polyester fiberfill to the size and shape of the inner line on pattern. Knot off, but do not break thread. Sew nose to face.

Step 4. Sew on oval button eyes.

Step 5. Trace mouse's scarf on paper side of fusible web. Cut out, leaving roughly $1/4$-inch margin around traced lines. Following manufacturer's instructions, fuse to contrasting single-face fleece. Cut out on traced lines. Referring to photo, position scarf on bag front and fuse.

Machine satin-stitch around side and lower edges with matching thread.

Step 6. From contrasting single-face fleece, cut two rectangles 12 x 2 inches. Right sides facing, sew the two rectangles together on both long sides. Turn right side out; press. Tie a single knot in the center and make ¹/₂-inch perpendicular clips ¹/₄ inch apart on each end for fringe.

Step 7. Sew face to bag as in Bunny Step 13. Tack knot of scarf in place below chin. If you choose to add a ribbon closure, do so as in Bunny Step 16.

Step 8. Thread long needle with white quilting thread for whiskers. Refer to **Fig. 2** for stitch placement. Insert needle at A and go out at B, leaving a 2-inch tail on the A side. Go back in near B, out at A, back in near A and out at B. Cut a 2-inch whisker on the B side to balance with whisker on the A side. Repeat twice, each time a little lower. The end result will be three whiskers each side of the nose.

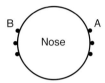

Fig. 2 Stitch whiskers for mouse as shown.

Step 9. Use cosmetic blush and a light hand to carefully apply blush to centers of ears. ▪

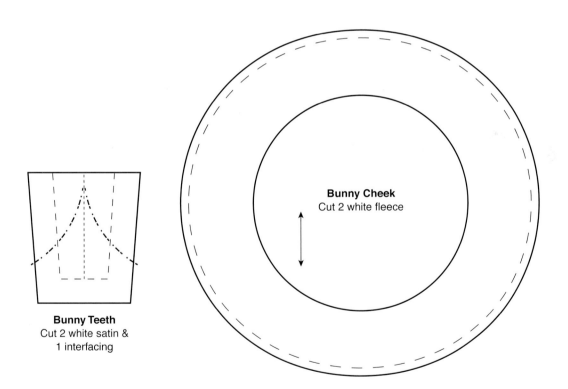

Bunny Teeth
Cut 2 white satin &
1 interfacing

Bunny Cheek
Cut 2 white fleece

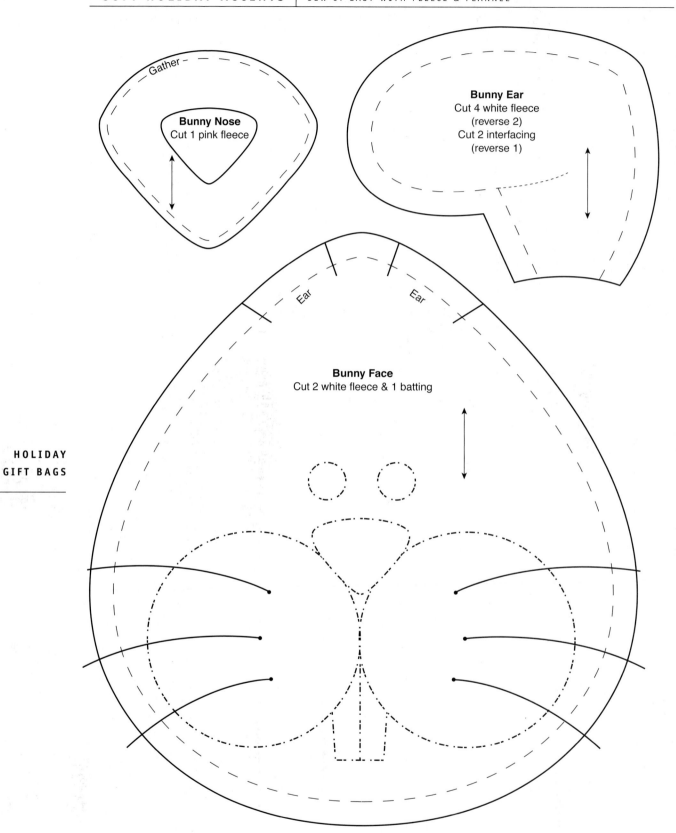

Gather

Bunny Nose
Cut 1 pink fleece

Bunny Ear
Cut 4 white fleece
(reverse 2)
Cut 2 interfacing
(reverse 1)

Ear   Ear

Bunny Face
Cut 2 white fleece & 1 batting

HOLIDAY
GIFT BAGS

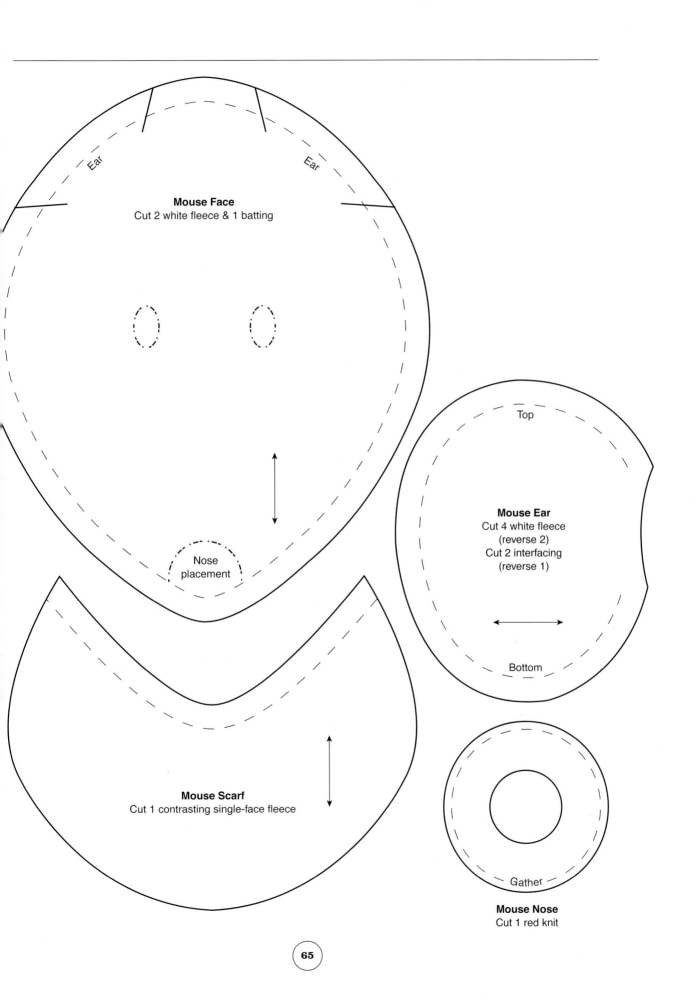

Mouse Face
Cut 2 white fleece & 1 batting

Ear

Ear

Nose
placement

Mouse Scarf
Cut 1 contrasting single-face fleece

Top

Mouse Ear
Cut 4 white fleece
(reverse 2)
Cut 2 interfacing
(reverse 1)

Bottom

Gather

Mouse Nose
Cut 1 red knit

Soft Angelic Pair By Sheri McCrimmon

Angels so soft, easy and adorable you'll always want to make them in pairs!

Project Specifications
Skill Level: Beginner
Angel Size: Approximately $4^1/_2$ x 7 inches

Materials
Note: *Materials are for two angels.*
- 2 white fleece squares 7 x 7 inches
- 2 white fleece squares 8 x 8 inches
- 2 round-top clothespins
- Two 7-inch lengths of 1-inch-wide lace
- 4 ($^1/_4$-inch) white pompoms
- 2 ($^1/_2$-inch) star or heart buttons
- Curly hair scraps or yarn scraps
- 2 ($^3/_4$-inch) gold wedding rings as found in wedding favor department of craft store
- Two 6-inch lengths of $^1/_8$-inch-wide metallic gold cord
- Two 4-inch lengths of pearl string
- Cotton swab
- Low-temperature glue gun
- Small paintbrush
- Skin-tone acrylic paint
- All-purpose white thread
- Fine-line black permanent marker
- Cosmetic blush
- Basic sewing supplies and tools

Instructions
Note: *Instructions are for one angel.*

Step 1. With small paint brush and skin-tone acrylic paint, paint rounded heads of clothespins and allow to dry.

Step 2. Pinch scraps of curly hair or yarn into small thumb-sized piles and glue to tops of clothespin heads with low-temperature glue gun. It is better to use more hair than you think necessary and trim after gluing.

Step 3. Sew one edge of 1-inch-wide lace to wrong side of one 7 x 7-inch white flannel square, which will make one dress. Fold the square in half, right sides facing, lace at bottom, and sew a seam from the top down through the lace with $^1/_2$-inch seam allowance. Turn right side out and cut fringe around top edge of dress. Cuts should be about $^1/_4$ inch wide and $1^1/_2$ inches deep into the fleece.

Step 4. With needle and thread, gather the top edge of the dress just below the fringe cuts.

Step 5. Place clothespin inside of dress and pull up thread. The seam of the dress should be at center back and the gathering line should be at angel neckline. Wrap thread around dress and clothespin a few times and knot. Glue to neck to secure.

Step 6. Make a small pinch at the dress center front, waist level, and glue to form arms. Glue two $^1/_4$-inch pompoms at the pinch for hands. Glue a heart or star button above the hands.

Step 7. Smooth fringe down over top of dress to reveal angel's face.

Step 8. For wings, fold one 8 x 8-inch white fleece square in half. Round the corners. Pinch the middle of the square together until it re-sembles a bow. Tack the pinched area together with needle and thread. Cut fringe through both layers, about $1/4$ inch wide. Make $1^{1}/_{4}$-inch cuts along the sides and $1/2$-inch cuts at the bottom.

Step 9. Wrap pearl strings around middle of wings and glue on one side.

Step 10. Fold $1/8$-inch-wide gold metallic cord in half and glue open edges to dress, just below fringe on back.

Step 11. Glue the middle of the wings to the back of the angel over the ribbon, with glued edges of pearl string against the back of the dress.

Step 12. Glue halo (wedding ring) to back of head at an angle, so it will stand up as shown in photo.

Step 13. With fine-line permanent marker make two small dots for eyes. Use cotton swab to apply cosmet-ic blush to cheeks.

Step 14. Repeat Steps 3–13 for second angel. ■

Snowflake Table Topper

By Carol Zentgraf

Bring on the hot chocolate and cookies! This is a perfect cold-weather table accessory.

Project Specifications
Skill Level: Beginner
Table Topper Size: Approximately 42 x 42 inches (including fringe)

Materials
- 1 yard coordinating plaid flannel
- 2 yards snowflake print flannel
- 4³/₄ yards white pompom fringe
- Rotary-cutting tools
- All-purpose threads to match fabrics
- Basic sewing supplies and tools

Instructions
Note: *Use a ¹/₄-inch seam allowance and sew right sides together unless otherwise indicated.*

Step 1. From snowflake print flannel, cut a 42-inch square for back of table topper. Cut three strips 6¹/₂ x 18 inches for the patchwork border. Cut four triangles, each with 22-inch sides and a 30 ⁷/₈-inch base.

Step 2. From the plaid flannel, cut one square 24 x 24 inches for the table topper center. Cut two strips 6¹/₂ x 18 inches for the patchwork border.

Step 3. For the patchwork border, sew the long edges of the 6¹/₂ x 18-inch strips together, beginning and ending with snowflake print. Press the seams open.

Step 4. Cut four 3¹/₂-inch-wide border strips across the width of the pieced panel as shown in **Fig. 1**.

Step 5. Remove one piece from the end of two border strips to make a four-piece strip. Sew these strips to opposite edges of the plaid center square. Press the seams open. Sew the five-piece border strips to the two remaining edges. Press seams open.

Step 6. Center and sew the base of one snowflake triangle to each side of the square. Press seams open. Trim edges, if necessary, to 42 x 42-inch square.

Step 7. Place the back of the table topper and the pieced front together, right sides facing. Sew around perimeter, leaving an opening for turning.

Step 8. Turn right side out and press. Close opening with hand stitches.

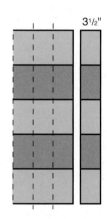

Fig. 1 Cut 4 strips 3¹/₂" wide as shown.

Step 9. Sew pompom fringe header to front edges of table topper with zigzag stitch.

Step 10. Use a snowflake or other decorative machine stitch to sew along both sides of the border strips. Cut four pompoms from the fringe header and sew one to each inner corner of border as shown in photo. ∎

Fleur-de-lis Valentine Centerpiece By Marian Shenk

Hearts, added to this fleur-de-lis variation, make this table topper a romantic attraction.

Project Specifications
Skill Level: Beginner
Centerpiece Size: Approximately 27$\frac{1}{2}$ x
    19$\frac{1}{2}$ inches

Materials
- Red fleece 25 x 17 inches
- 1 yard white fleece
- Red and white all-purpose thread
- $\frac{3}{4}$ yard fusible web
- 3 yards $\frac{3}{8}$-inch-wide white lace edging
- Pattern paper
- Basic sewing supplies and tools

Instructions
Step 1. Cut two white fleece rectangles 28 x 20 inches. Fold each piece in quarters and round corners as shown in **Fig. 1** to make two ovals.

Step 2. Fold red fleece in quarters. Place scallop pattern on folds and cut on scallop lines.

Step 3. Center red scalloped oval on one white fleece oval. With red thread, satin-stitch around scallops to secure.

Step 4. Fold fusible web in quarters. Open flat on work surface. Place fleur-de-lis pattern on paper folds and flip and trace pattern to make four fleur-de-lis shapes. Also trace eight hearts

on paper side of fusible web. Cut out shapes, leaving roughly 1/4 inch around traced lines.

Step 5. Following manufacturer's instructions, fuse pieces to wrong side of white fleece. Cut out on traced lines and peel off paper.

Step 6. Referring to photo for placement, arrange fleur-de-lis and heart shapes on scalloped red center; fuse.

Step 7. With white thread, satin-stitch around shapes.

Step 8. Place lace edging around the outside of the appliquéd oval, right sides facing, edges aligned.

Step 9. Place second white fleece oval on top of appliquéd oval. Sew around perimeter with 1/4-inch seam allowance, leaving 4-inch opening for turning.

Step 10. Turn right side out; press. Close opening with hand stitches. ▨

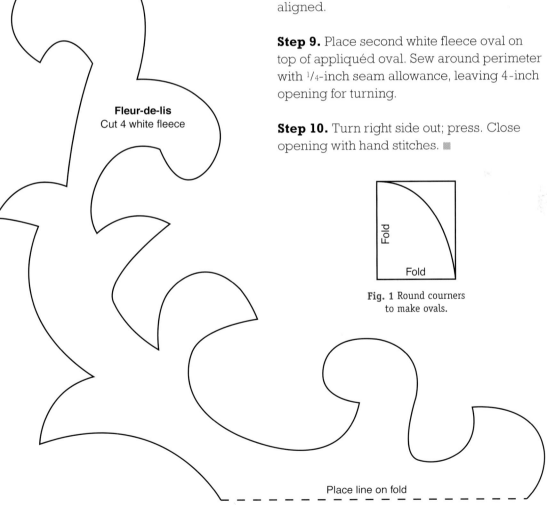

Fleur-de-lis
Cut 4 white fleece

Fold

Fold

Fig. 1 Round courners to make ovals.

Place line on fold

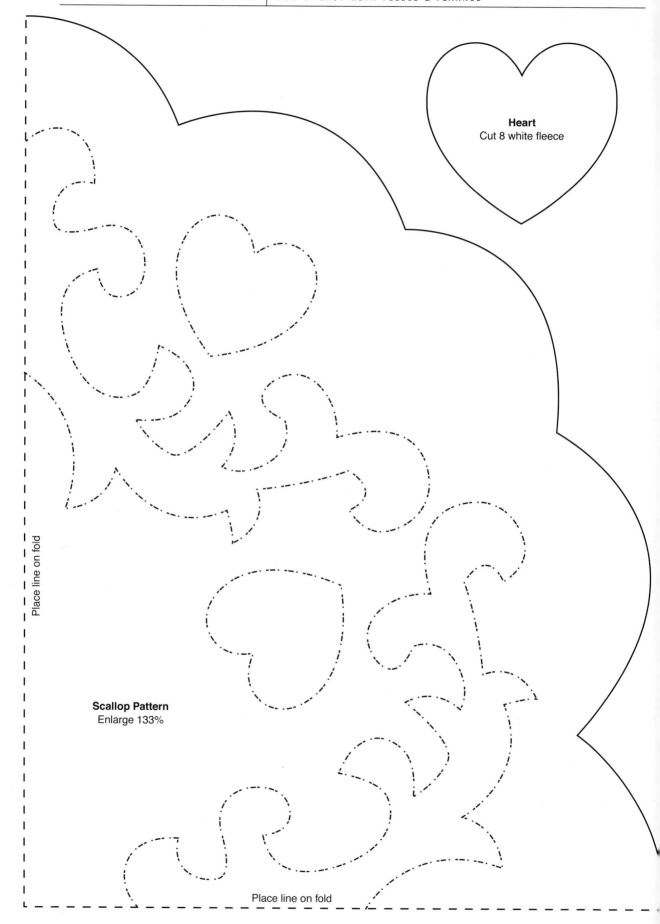

Heart
Cut 8 white fleece

Place line on fold

Scallop Pattern
Enlarge 133%

Place line on fold

Pumpkin Pullover
By Carol Zentgraf

What fun to be turned into a pumpkin!

Project Specifications
Skill Level: Beginner
Pullover Size: Any size

Materials
- Commercial pullover pattern designed for fleece
- Orange fleece in yardage indicated on pattern for selected size
- Enough black fleece to cut one pullover front in size selected
- Water-soluble marker
- Tracing paper

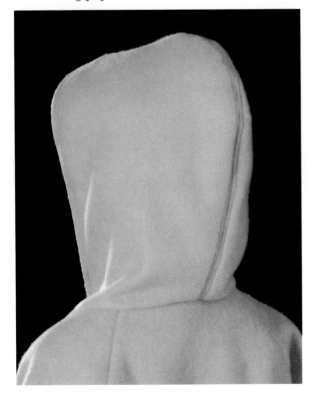

- Orange all-purpose thread
- Small, sharp-pointed scissors
- Quilt basting spray
- Basic sewing supplies and tools

Instructions
Step 1. Follow pattern guide sheet to cut pullover pieces from orange fleece. Cut one front piece from black fleece.

Step 2. With right sides up and edges aligned, place the orange front piece on the black front piece. Baste the edges together.

Step 3. Trace the pumpkin eyes and nose pattern three times on tracing paper. Trace pumpkin mouth on tracing paper. Cut patterns out on traced lines.

Step 4. Following manufacturer's instructions, lightly spray the back of each pattern piece with quilt basting spray. Referring to photo for placement, arrange and adhere to orange pullover front.

Step 5. Stitch around each pattern piece $1/8$ inch from the edge of the pattern. Remove the pattern pieces and carefully cut through the orange fleece layer only, $1/8$ inch from the stitching line.

Step 6. Complete pullover following pattern directions. ■

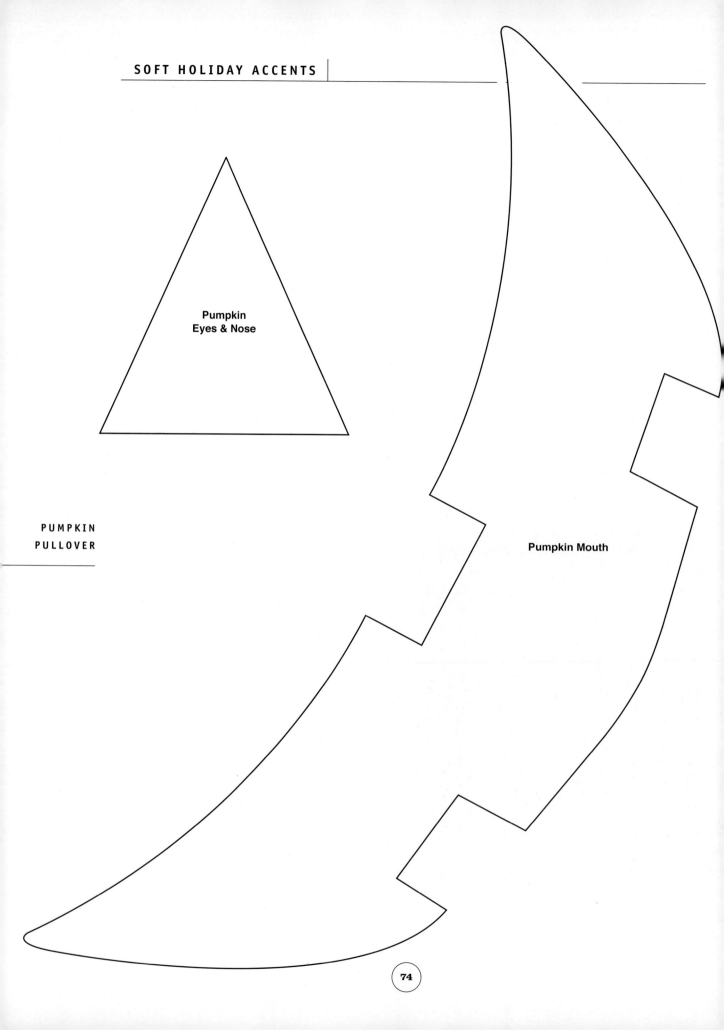

Pumpkin
Eyes & Nose

PUMPKIN
PULLOVER

Pumpkin Mouth

Soft & Cuddly Bunny By Marian Shenk

Who could resist this adorable, cuddly friend?

Project Specifications
Skill Level: Beginner
Bunny Size: Approximately 20 x 16 inches

Materials
- Simplicity pattern #9524, view B
- $1/4$ yard lavender fleece for vest
- $1/4$ yard coordinating flannel for vest lining
- $3/4$ yard 60-inch-wide white fleece
- $2^1/4$ yards $3/4$-inch-wide lavender lace
- 2 ($5/8$-inch) craft eyes
- Black 6-strand embroidery floss
- $2^1/2$ yards $3/4$-inch-wide lavender satin ribbon
- Polyester fiberfill in amount recommended on pattern
- White and lavender all-purpose thread
- Basic sewing supplies and tools

Instructions
Step 1. Follow the commercial pattern to construct the bunny.

Step 2. Cut vest and lining pieces as instructed on patterns.

Step 3. Sew fleece vest together at sides. Sew vest lining pieces together at sides.

Step 4. Pin $3/4$-inch-wide lace along front and back lower edges and around armholes. Place lining right sides together with vest and stitch edges where lace is pinned. Clip seams on curves. Turn right side out; press.

Step 5. Sew shoulder seams together. Sew lace around neckline edge.

Step 6. Cut 1 yard of $3/4$-inch-wide lavender satin ribbon. Fold in half and use as binding over raw edges of neckline. Start binding at center back and work to front edges. Place vest on bunny and tie ends of ribbon in a bow.

Step 7. Cut remaining lavender ribbon in half and tie a bow on each ear as shown in photo.

Step 8. From white fleece, cut one tail. Fold on centerline and sew curved raw edges. Turn right side out and stuff with polyester fiberfill. Stitch to lower back of bunny. ■

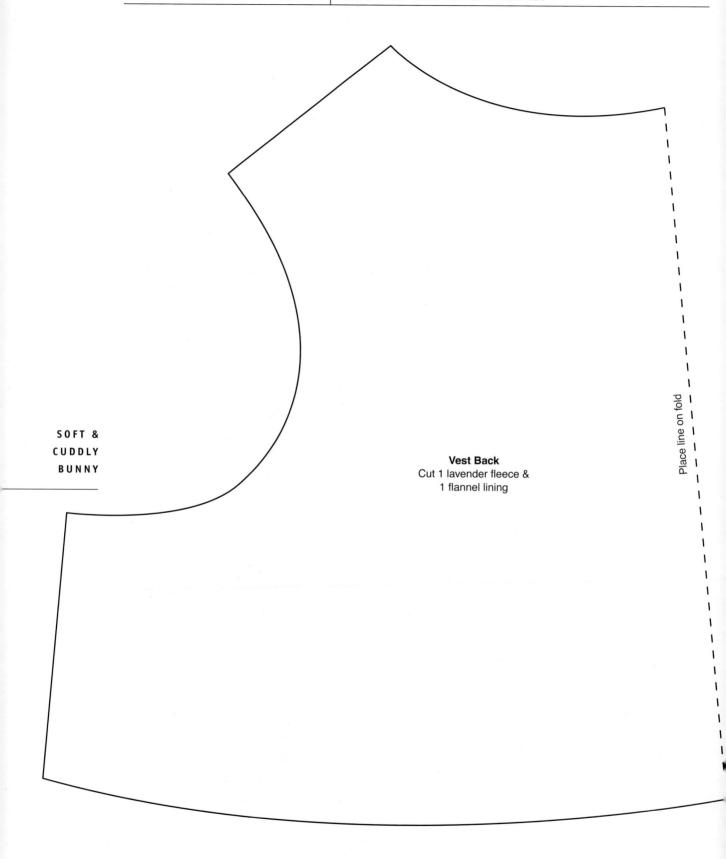

**SOFT &
CUDDLY
BUNNY**

Vest Back
Cut 1 lavender fleece &
1 flannel lining

Place line on fold

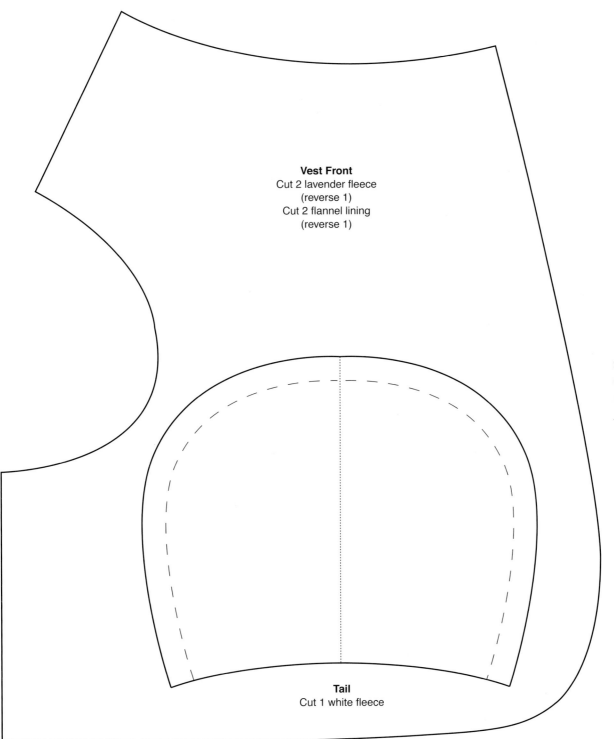

Vest Front
Cut 2 lavender fleece
(reverse 1)
Cut 2 flannel lining
(reverse 1)

Tail
Cut 1 white fleece

Eggs-ceptional Place Mats
By Carol Zentgraf

Reversible place mats—one side for Easter dining and the other side perfect for year-round use.

Project Specifications
Skill Level: Beginner
Place Mat Size: Approximately 19 x 13 inches

Materials
Note: *Materials and instructions are for one place mat.*
- Scraps of three coordinating flannel checks for appliqué
- 2 contrasting plaid flannel rectangles 19 x 13 inches
- Coordinating floral flannel bias strip 2¼ x 45 inches for binding
- Fusible batting rectangle 19 x 13 inches
- 3 pieces fusible web 3 x 4 inches
- Tear-away stabilizer 6 x 8 inches
- Permanent fabric adhesive

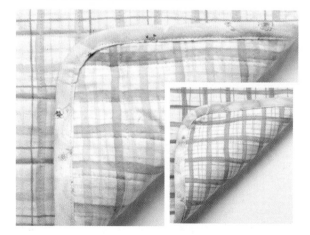

- Shaggy novelty yarn for trim
- All-purpose threads to match fabrics
- Rayon embroidery thread to match appliqués
- Rotary-cutting tools
- Basic sewing supplies and tools

Instructions
Step 1. Trace egg on paper side of fusible web as directed on pattern. Cut out, leaving roughly ¼ inch around traced lines.

Step 2. Following manufacturer's instructions, fuse eggs to selected appliqué scraps. Cut out on traced lines.

Step 3. Referring to photo, position eggs on lower left corner of one plaid flannel rectangle; fuse.

Step 4. Pin tear-away stabilizer to reverse side of appliqué area. With rayon embroidery thread and a 5.0-wide satin stitch, machine-stitch around the eggs.

Step 5. Sandwich fusible batting rectangle between the wrong sides of the two plaid rectangles, aligning the edges; fuse.

Step 6. With matching all-purpose thread in the needle and bobbin, stitch along the

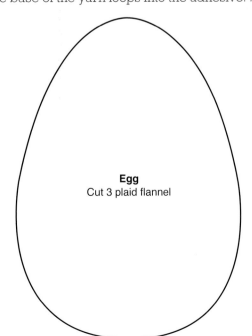

horizontal and vertical plaid lines of your choice to quilt the place mat.

Step 7. If necessary, trim the edges even and square the corners. Cut one corner into a curve, then use the corner as a guide to cut the three remaining corners.

Step 8. To bind the edges of the place mat, sew binding to place mat, right sides together, raw edges aligned. Start sewing at the center of the place mat's front lower edge, turning the end of the bias strip under. Sew around the perimeter, overlapping the ends.

Step 9. Press the binding to the backside of the place mat. On the backside of the mat, turn the binding edge under 1/2 inch and press in place, covering the first stitching line. From the right side of the place mat, stitch in the ditch along the binding, making certain the binding on the back is caught in the stitching.

Step 10. To add grass to the appliquéd eggs, shape a doubled length of shaggy novelty yarn into loops. Apply a thin line of permanent fabric adhesive along the base of the eggs and press the base of the yarn loops into the adhesive. ■

Egg
Cut 3 plaid flannel

Holiday Spirt Vest Continued from page 52

to photo for placement, use a double strand of black all-purpose sewing thread and sew the pieces to two of the pockets with large, irregular-length primitive running stitches.

Step 7. Trace and cut heart shapes as directed on patterns. Sew to remaining two pockets as in Step 6.

Step 8. Position a pocket on each side of the vest 2 inches from the center edge and 1½ inches from the lower edge. Mark the button placements through the buttonholes. Remove the pockets and sew a ½-inch silver button to each mark.

Step 9. Button pockets in place. Cut strips of hook-and-loop to fit the side and lower edges of each pocket. Use fabric glue to adhere the loop side of the strips to the vest under each pocket. Glue the hook side to the pocket edges. Cut another set of hook strips and glue to the remaining two pockets with heart shapes. ■

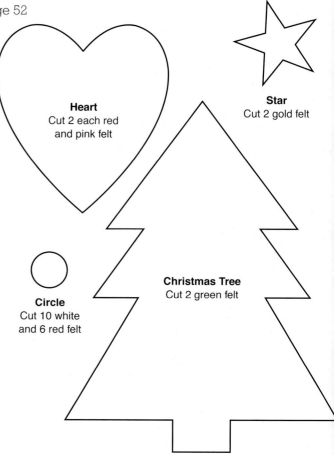

Heart
Cut 2 each red
and pink felt

Star
Cut 2 gold felt

Circle
Cut 10 white
and 6 red felt

Christmas Tree
Cut 2 green felt

Festive Christmas Place Mats
Continued from page 58

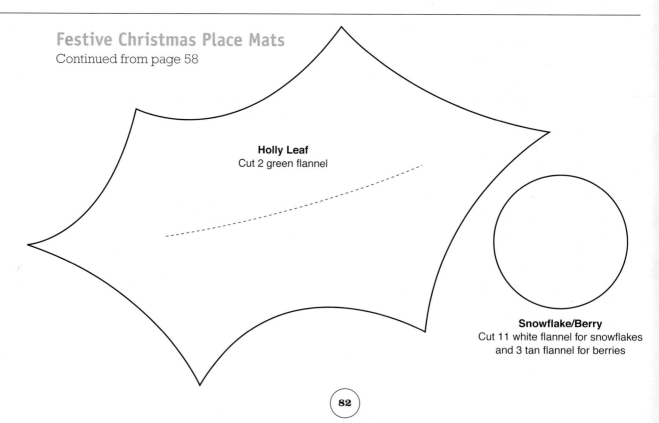

Holly Leaf
Cut 2 green flannel

Snowflake/Berry
Cut 11 white flannel for snowflakes
and 3 tan flannel for berries

COMFY AT HOME

Traditionally, fleece and flannel garments have been comfortable clothes in which to relax or sleep. Today's fabrics are more comfy than ever before.

Shimmering Strands Kimono

By Nancy Fiedler

Decorative threads couched on flannel create a garment with a lot of pizzazz!

Project Specifications
Skill Level: Intermediate
Kimono Size: Any size

Materials
- Commercial kimono pattern (Simplicity pattern 7183 used for model)
- Flannel in amount suggested on pattern plus an additional $1/2$ yard
- $1^1/2$ yards contrasting flannel for bands and sash
- Lining fabric in amount suggested on pattern
- $5^1/4$ yards 22-inch-wide fusible knit interfacing
- YLI Multi's Embellishment yarn in colors that coordinate with flannel
- YLI Candlelight metallic yarn in assorted colors that coordinate with flannel
- Assorted embroidery threads in colors that coordinate with flannel
- All-purpose thread that matches fabrics
- Multi-cording foot to fit sewing machine
- $^{11}/_{75}$ needles
- Basic sewing supplies and tools

Instructions
Step 1. Prewash and press flannel. Lay out the main pattern pieces and cut pieces of flannel for each pattern piece that are 2 inches larger all the way around. Fuse the knit interfacing to the wrong side of each flannel piece.

Step 2. Embellish the flannel by couching decorative threads in random flowing lines of stitches on each of the flannel pieces. Refer to the photo for ideas. Experiment with the embellishing threads and stitches on scraps of flannel to perfect the look you want to achieve.

Step 3. To couch threads, attach the multi-cording foot on your sewing machine. Place one or more strands of the embellishing yarns in the foot. Thread the machine with embroidery thread. For a single yarn, set the machine for a zigzag stitch that is the width of the yarn and sew the yarn in random rows down the length of the flannel. When using multiple strands of yarn, select a stitch that will catch each yarn, such as a three-step zigzag or herringbone stitch. Add interest to the couched yarns by selecting one of the machine's built-in decorative stitches, but make sure the stitch catches all the yarns. As seen in the photo, multiple yarns were couched to achieve a multicolored effect.

Step 4. When all of the embellishment is complete, press all flannel pieces from the wrong side.

Step 5. Cut out all of the pattern pieces. To make the contrasting cuffs on the sleeves,

Continued on page 116

Dog's Stamp of Approval

By Carol Zentgraf

Keep your favorite pup warm with a personalized, cozy fleece coat.

Project Specifications
Skill Level: Beginner
Dog Coat Size: Any size

Materials
- Commercial dog coat pattern (Kwik Sew pattern 2879 used for model)
- Fleece and cotton lining in yardage recommended on pattern
- 8 x 8-inch square of contrasting cotton print for bone
- Interfacing and hook-and-loop tape as recommended on pattern
- 4 x 8-inch rectangle of fusible web
- 8 x 8-inch square of fusible vinyl
- All-purpose threads to match fabrics
- Clear polymer paw-print stamp
- Black textile paint
- Fabric ink pad
- Basic sewing supplies and tools

Instructions
Step 1. Like people, dogs don't always fit standard sizes, so fit the pattern pieces to your pet before cutting them. Measure from the base of the neckline to the base of the tail to determine length. Measure around the neck to determine the front closure and collar length. Measure across the chest to determine the strap length.

Step 2. Follow the pattern instructions to cut out the coat, collar and strap pieces from fleece and cotton lining fabrics. Cut a collar from interfacing.

Step 3. Place fleece pieces on work surface for stamping. Pour a small amount of black textile paint onto the fabric ink pad. Work the paint into the pad using the back of a spoon. Tap the stamp onto the ink pad until the surface is evenly covered, but not saturated. Hold the stamp by the edges and press it straight down on the fabric. Use the fingers of your other hand to press it evenly onto the surface. Lift the stamp straight up without sliding it. Repeat randomly on all three pieces. Let paint dry overnight.

Step 4. Follow pattern instructions to make coat and to apply hook-and-loop tape to the strap and front closure.

Step 5. Trace bone pattern on paper side of fusible web. Cut out roughly around shape. Following manufacturer's instructions, fuse to 8 x 8-inch square of contrasting cotton print. Cut out on traced lines. Remove paper backing and fuse to remaining matching fabric. Cut edges even with first bone to make double-sided bone.

Step 6. Cut two 4 x 8-inch pieces of fusible vinyl. Following the manufacturer's instructions, sandwich the fabric bone between two vinyl pieces and fuse. Cut out along edge of vinyl-coated bone.

Step 7. Topstitch close to the edge of the vinyl-coated bone. Fasten the front closure and center the bone horizontally across the edge; pin to the overlap. Open the closure and zigzag-stitch the center of the bone in place along both edges. ■

DOG'S
STAMP OF
APPROVAL

Bone

Teen Pajama Pants & Top

By Carol Zentgraf

Not only are these pajamas cute and trendy, they are simple enough for a teen to sew by herself!

Project Specifications

Skill Level: Beginner
Pajama Size: Any size

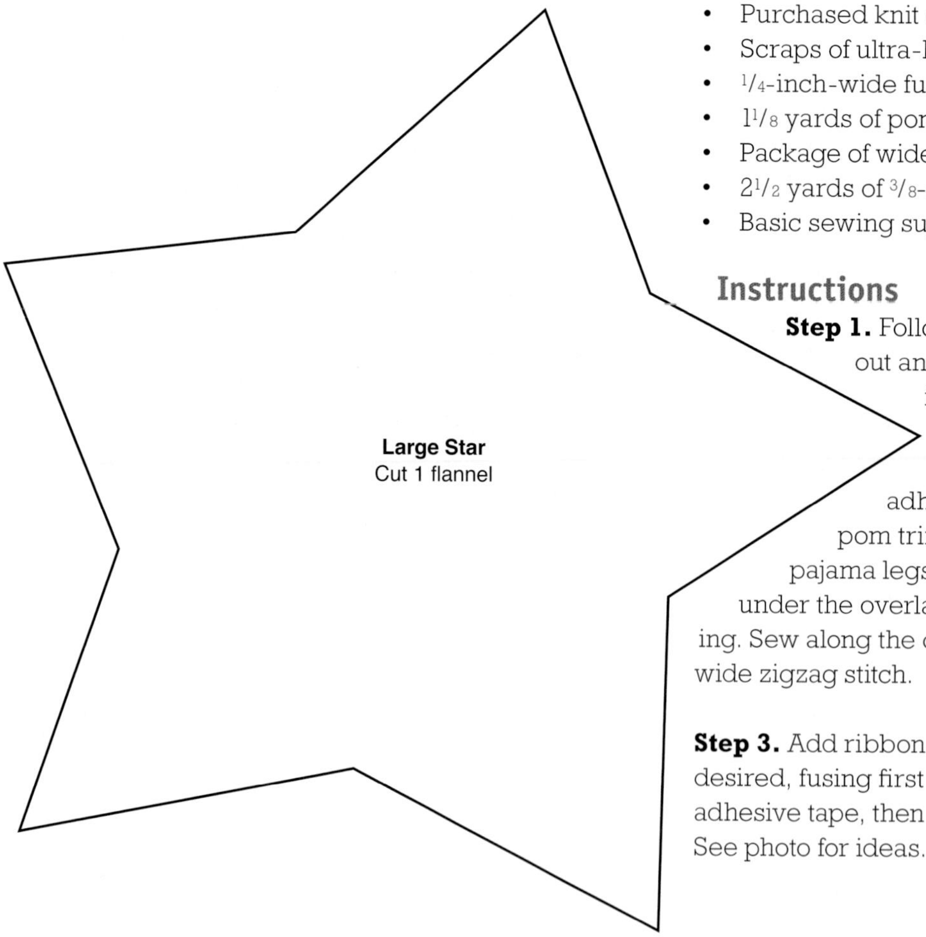

Large Star
Cut 1 flannel

Materials

- Commercial pajama pants pattern
- Flannel in yardage recommended on pattern
- Notions as recommended on pattern
- Purchased knit camisole
- Scraps of ultra-hold fusible web
- $1/4$-inch-wide fusible adhesive tape
- $1^1/8$ yards of pompom trim
- Package of wide rickrack
- $2^1/2$ yards of $3/8$-inch-wide satin ribbon
- Basic sewing supplies and tools

Instructions

Step 1. Follow pattern instructions to cut out and sew pajama pants from flannel.

Step 2. Use $1/4$-inch-wide adhesive tape to adhere pompom trim to the lower edge of the pajama legs. Overlap the ends, turning under the overlapping end to prevent raveling. Sew along the center of the trim tape with a wide zigzag stitch.

Step 3. Add ribbon and rickrack trim as desired, fusing first with $1/2$-inch-wide fusible adhesive tape, then sewing with a straight stitch. See photo for ideas.

Step 4. Cut a 28-inch length of ³/₈-inch-wide satin ribbon.

Step 5. Trace small stars on paper side of ultra-hold fusible web as instructed on pattern. Cut out, leaving roughly ¹/₄-inch margin around traced lines.

Step 6. Following manufacturer's instructions, fuse to flannel fabric. Cut out on traced lines.

Step 7. Place two stars together, sandwiching end of 28-inch ribbon between. Fuse two stars together, ribbon enclosed. Repeat on other end of ribbon.

Step 8. Tie an off-center bow with 2¹/₂-inch loops. Stitch the center of the bow to the waistband at center front.

Step 9. To embellish the camisole, use ¹/₄-inch-wide fusible adhesive tape to adhere rickrack to the lower edge and ribbon at the front neckline as shown in photo. Stitch trims in place with straight stitch.

Step 10. Trace large star on paper side of ultra-hold fusible web. Cut out roughly around traced lines and fuse to flannel. Cut out on traced lines. Remove paper backing and fuse to the center of the camisole, 1 inch below the ribbon trim. ■

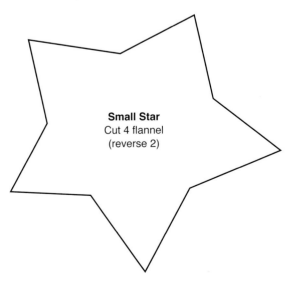

Small Star
Cut 4 flannel
(reverse 2)

Fluffy Fleece Bathrobe
By Carol Zentgraf

You'll experience head-to-toe coziness when you snuggle up in this very feminine robe.

Project Specifications
Skill Level: Beginner
Bathrobe Size: Any size

Materials
- Commercial bathrobe pattern designed for fleece (Kwik Sew #2727 used for model)
- Fleece in yardage required by pattern
- Notions as required by pattern
- 2 packages of Chenille by the Inch in contrasting color
- Chenille by the Inch cutting guide
- Chenille brush
- Perforated tear-away stabilizer
- Spray water bottle

- Acrylic ruler with 45-degree-angle marks
- Rotary-cutting tools
- Basic sewing supplies and tools

Instructions
Step 1. Follow the pattern guide sheet to cut the bathrobe pattern pieces from fleece.

Step 2. On the center front edge of the bathrobe front pattern piece, measure 12¼ inches down from the neckline and mark. Draw a line across the pattern perpendicular to the center front to create a bodice pattern. Use this bodice pattern to cut two bodice pieces from the perforated tear-away stabilizer. Mark a ¼-inch seam allowance on the neck and front edges of each stabilizer piece.

Step 3. Mark the front edge of each bodice stabilizer piece at 4-inch intervals as shown in **Fig. 1**. Use the 45-degree-angle mark on the acrylic ruler to draw the diagonal grid lines from the marks as shown in **Fig. 2**.

Step 4. Pin each stabilizer piece to a fleece bathrobe front, making certain the marks match at the center front edges.

Step 5. Remove the stabilizer from the back of the Chenille by the Inch. Use the cutting guide and a rotary cutter to cut the strips between the stitching lines. Align the stitch of the chenille strips with the marked lines on the stabilizer and stitch the chenille strips in place, overlapping the strip ends ¼ inch as needed.

Step 6. Lightly spray the chenille strips with water and brush until fluffy; let dry. Tear away the stabilizer.

Step 7. Follow the pattern instructions to complete the robe, being careful to align the chenille design at the zipper edges. ■

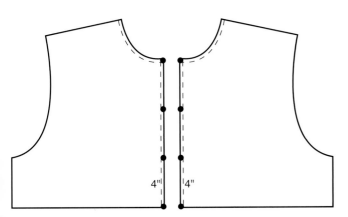

Fig. 1 Mark center front at 4" intervals as shown.

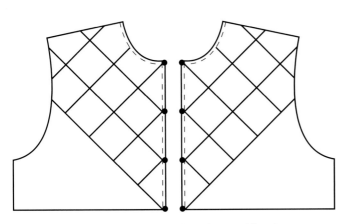

Fig. 2 Use acrylic ruler to mark 45-degree grid as shown.

Star Overnight Backpack
By Holly Daniels

Send your happy traveler off to a sleepover in style!

Project Specifications
Skill Level: Beginner
Backpack Size: Approximately 18 x 18 inches
Cosmetic Bag Size: 6^1/$_4$ x 7^1/$_2$ inches

Materials
- ^{1}/$_2$ yard blue star-print flannel
- 1^1/$_4$ yards yellow flannel
- 14 x 14-inch square of tear-away stabilizer
- All-purpose threads to match fabrics
- 14-inch yellow zipper for backpack
- 9-inch blue zipper for cosmetic bag
- 1 yard ^{3}/$_4$-inch-wide elastic
- Basic sewing supplies and tools

Instructions

BACKPACK

Step 1. From yellow flannel, cut one large star. From blue star-print flannel, cut one small star.

Step 2. Layer tear-away stabilizer, large star and small star; pin.

Step 3. With machine satin stitch, sew small blue star to yellow star. Tear away the stabilizer.

Step 4. Cut two pieces of yellow flannel 11 x 20 inches for back. Place right sides together and machine-baste a ^{1}/$_2$-inch seam along one long edge. Press seam open.

Step 5. Place a pin 3 inches from one end of seam as shown in **Fig. 1**. Place 14-inch yellow zipper against seam allowances with top of

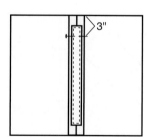

Fig. 1 Place pin 3" from end
of seam as shown.

zipper against pin. Align zipper coils with seam. Baste zipper to seam allowance. Stitch $1/4$ inch each side of seam. Press lightly from right side. Remove basting stitches.

Step 6. From yellow flannel, cut a 3 x 2-inch rectangle. Press the raw edges under $1/4$ inch on both long and one short side. Place over the opening at the top of the zipper and baste in place. Machine-stitch using a $1/4$-inch seam allowance as shown in **Fig. 2**; press.

Step 7. Layer the star front and the zippered back, right sides facing. The zipper should run down the center of the star and the zipper pull should rest about $2^1/2$ inches below the raw edge of the top of the star. Pin all raw edges around the star. Open zipper slightly.

Step 8. Sew the star to the back using a $1/4$-inch seam allowance. The end of the zipper will intersect the bottom of the star. Sew over this area carefully. Trim away any excess zipper.

Step 9. Trim the back to match the front seam allowance. Clip corners and curves. Open zipper and turn right side out.

Step 10. From yellow flannel, cut two strips $2^1/2$ x 24 inches. Fold each strip in half lengthwise and sew with $1/4$-inch seam allowance, forming long tubes. Turn each tube right side out.

STAR OVERNIGHT BACKPACK

Step 11. Cut $3/4$-inch-wide elastic in half. Thread one piece through each tube, securing at each end with a line of machine stitches.

Step 12. Fold over each end of elastic straps to enclose raw edges. Sew to back of backpack as indicated in **Fig. 3**.

COSMETIC BAG

Step 1. From blue star-print flannel, cut two rectangles 8 x 7 inches. Place right sides together. Machine-baste $1/2$ inch from one long edge. Press seam open.

Step 2. Place right side of 9-inch blue zipper against seam allowance, zipper coils aligned with seam. Baste zipper to seam allowance. Machine-stitch $1/4$ inch from seam. Press lightly from the right side. Remove basting stitches from seam.

Step 3. Fold the bag, right sides facing, and pin the seam allowances. Open the zipper slightly. Sew pinned edges with $1/4$-inch seam allowance. Trim excess fabric from the corners. Open zipper and turn bag right side out. ■

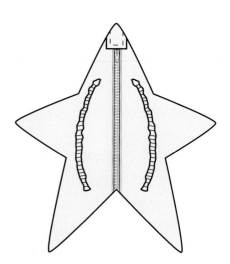

Fig. 3 Stitch elastic straps to backpack as shown.

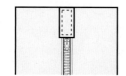

Fig. 2 Machine-stitch rectangle over opening at top of zipper.

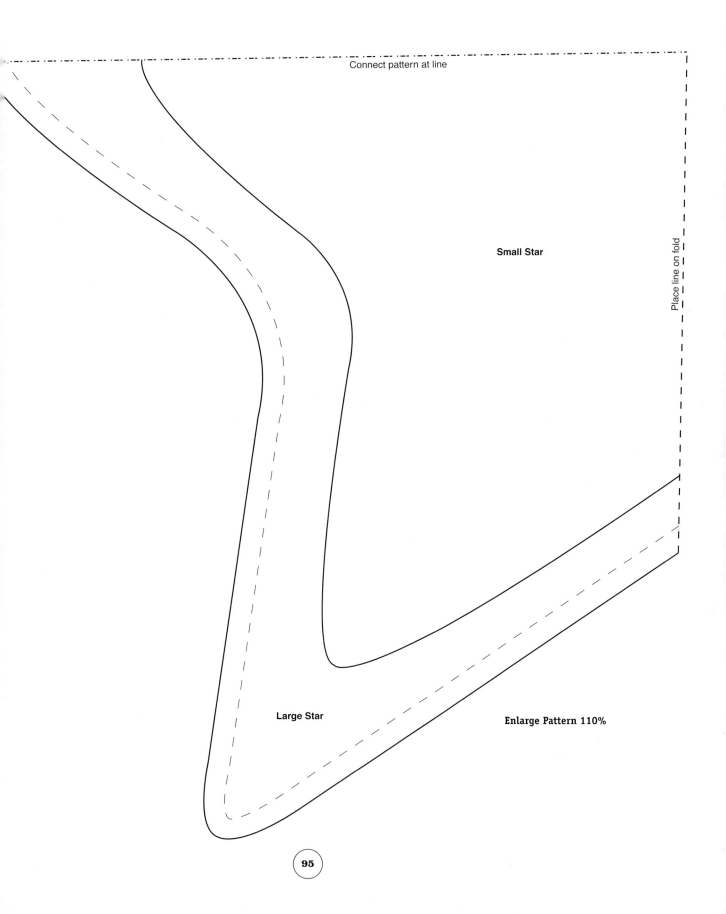

Connect pattern at line

Small Star

Place line on fold

Large Star

Enlarge Pattern 110%

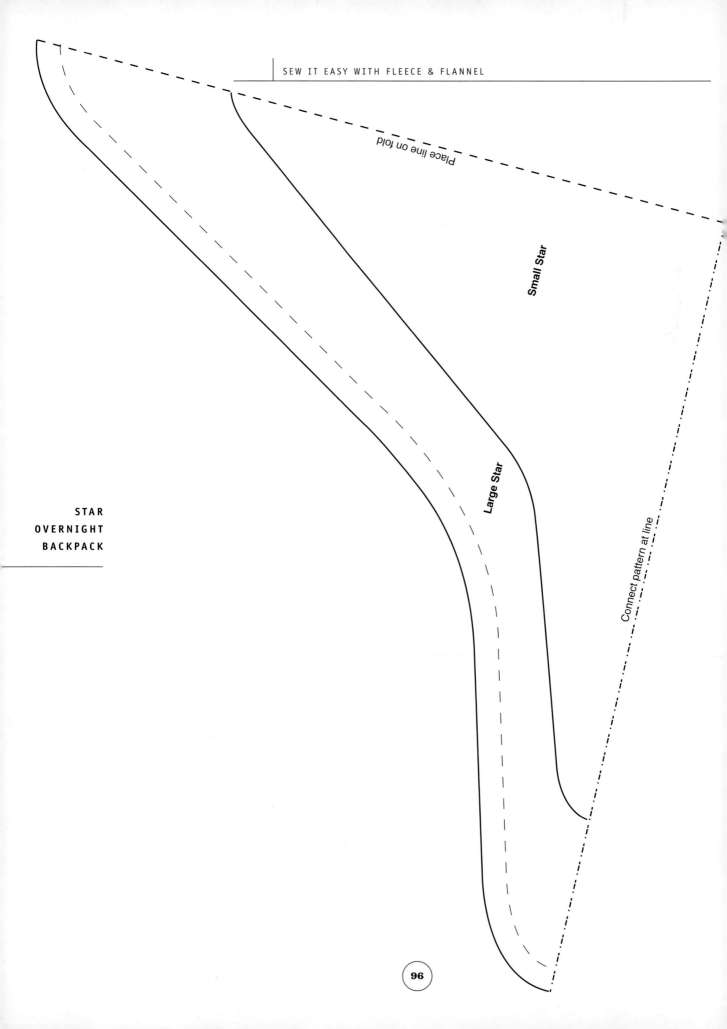

Place line on fold

Small Star

Large Star

Connect pattern at line

STAR
OVERNIGHT
BACKPACK

Autumn Leaves Throw
By Willow Ann Sirch

You'll be toasty warm under this bright throw when the leaves begin to color and the nights turn cool.

Project Specifications
Skill Level: Beginner
Throw Size: 48 x 48 inches

Materials
- Red and orange flannel scraps for appliqué
- $1/4$ yard each dark green, medium green, gold and rust calico-print flannels
- $1/2$ yard light green solid flannel
- 2 yards leaf-print flannel for blocks and borders
- 54 x 54-inch flannel backing
- 54 x 54-inch thin batting
- 6 yards $2^1/_2$-inch-wide flannel binding
- All-purpose threads to match fabrics
- Quilting thread
- Air-soluble marker
- Rotary-cutting tools
- Basic sewing supplies and tools

Instructions
Step 1. Prewash and press all fabrics.

Step 2. From the dark green, medium green, gold and rust calico print flannels, cut six squares each $4^1/_2$ x $4^1/_2$ inches. From the rust and gold calico print flannels, cut two squares each $6^1/_2$ x $6^1/_2$ inches.

Step 3. From the leaf print flannel, cut two border strips each $6^1/_2$ x $36^1/_2$ inches and $6^1/_2$ x $48^1/_2$ inches. Cut 24 squares $4^1/_2$ x $4^1/_2$ inches.

Step 4. With air-soluble marker, trace leaf shapes as instructed on templates. Referring to the photo for color placement, appliqué leaves to $6^1/_2$-inch squares.

Step 5. Sew appliqués squares together in a Four-Patch as shown in photo.

Step 6. From light green solid flannel, cut two strips each $2^1/_2$ x $12^1/_2$ inches and $2^1/_2$ x $16^1/_2$ inches. Sew two shorter strips to opposite sides of Four-Patch and longer strips to top and bottom.

Step 7. Combine two squares of each color of the $4^1/_2$-inch calico-print squares cut in Step 2 with two leaf print flannel squares to make 12 Four-Patch blocks as shown in **Fig. 1**.

Step 8. Referring to the photo, arrange the Four-Patch blocks around the center square. Sew blocks together in rows and then sew rows together.

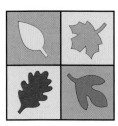

Fig. 1 Make 4-patch blocks with 2 calico-print squares and 2 leaf-print squares.

Step 9. From light green solid flannel, cut two strips each 2¹/₂ x 32¹/₂ inches and 2¹/₂ x 36¹/₂ inches. Sew the shorter strips to the top and bottom of the throw and the longer strips to the sides.

Step 10. Sew the shorter border strips cut in Step 3 to the top and bottom of the throw. Sew the longer strips to the sides.

Step 11. Sandwich the quilt top, batting and backing layers. Pin or baste the layers together.

Step 12. Quilt as desired by hand or machine.

Step 13. Bind quilt with 2¹/₂-inch flannel binding to finish. ■

AUTUMN LEAVES THROW

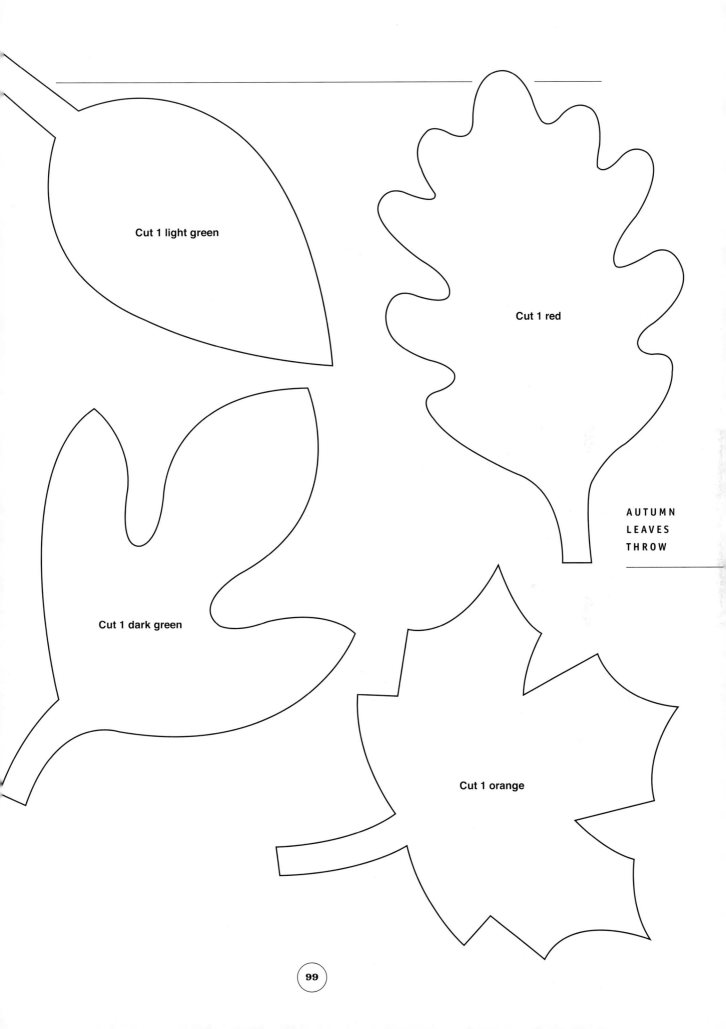

Cut 1 light green

Cut 1 red

Cut 1 dark green

AUTUMN
LEAVES
THROW

Cut 1 orange

Sunshine Bright Throw

By Pearl Louise Krush

Fun to make and fun to cuddle with!

Project Specifications
Skill Level: Beginner
Throw Size: Approximately 52 x 65 inches

Materials
- 3 yards each of 4 different homespun plaid flannels
- $1/2$ yard contrasting homespun plaid flannel for binding
- Rotary-cutting tools
- Sharp scissors
- Fabric softener sheet
- Basic sewing supplies and tools

Instructions
Step 1. Cut 20 squares 14 x 14 inches from each of the four different homespun plaid flannels.

Step 2. Decide which of the homespun plaids you want to use for the backing of the throw. Stack one each of the three remaining squares on top of each backing square. Make 20 stacks, each in the same order. ***Note:*** *Having a top fabric with a natural $1/2$-inch plaid will eliminate having to mark stitching lines on the fabrics.*

Step 3. Use safety pins in each block to hold all of the layers together.

Step 4. Sew diagonal $1/2$-inch seams across each entire block. Ideally, you will have a plaid to follow. If not, mark stitching lines or establish some means of stitching consistent lines $1/2$ inch apart.

Step 5. Carefully insert blades of scissors between the back layer and the top three layers between sewn lines. Cut through the top three layers of fabric between each seam. Repeat this process on all blocks.

Step 6. Arrange blocks on work surface, placing four blocks across in five rows. Using $1/2$-inch seam allowance, sew each row of blocks together with seams sewn up (wrong sides facing). Sew rows of blocks together.

Step 7. Clip seams perpendicular to the seam line at $1/2$-inch intervals.

Step 8. Cut contrasting homespun plaid in $2^{1}/_{2}$-inch strips across the width of the fabric. Sew the strips together end to end for binding.

Step 9. Fold the binding in half lengthwise, wrong sides facing; press. Bind quilt to finish.

Step 10. Place quilt in a cold-water wash. Remove any loose threads from washer.

Step 11. Place quilt in dryer with fabric softener sheet. Dry completely. Shake quilt out of doors to remove excess threads and lint. Remove threads from dryer periodically as quilt dries. ■

Homespuns used to make throw.

Floral Lattice Pillow By Marian Shenk

Decorating with fleece is fast and fun because there is no fussy finishing!

Project Specifications
Skill Level: Beginner
Pillow Size: 16 x 16 inches

Materials
- 17 x 17-inch square of print fleece for pillow top
- 17 x 17-inch square of coordinating solid-color fleece for pillow back
- ¹/₂ yard 60-inch-wide coordinating solid-color fleece for lattice and fringe
- 16-inch pillow form
- 6-strand embroidery floss that contrasts with lattice fabric
- All-purpose thread to match fabrics
- Pencil or marker
- Basic sewing supplies and tools

Instructions
Step 1. From 60-inch-wide coordinating solid-color fleece, cut six 1-inch-wide strips across the width of the fabric. Fold each strip in half lengthwise and zigzag the raw edges together. Fold seam to center back of strip and steam-press.

Step 2. On the 17 x 17-inch pillow top square, mark a diagonal grid as shown in **Fig. 1**.

Step 3. Place prepared lattice strips on marked grid, weaving them over and under until all lines are covered. Pin the strips to the pillow top.

Step 4. With 6 strands of contrasting embroidery floss, work a cross-stitch at each lattice intersection, securing to the pillow top.

Step 5. Machine-stitch around the perimeter of the pillow top to secure lattice strip ends. Trim strips even with pillow top.

Step 6. From 60-inch-wide coordinating solid-color fleece, cut four strips 17 x 3 inches for fringe. Place strips around perimeter of pillow front, right sides facing.

Step 7. Place backing square on pillow front, right sides facing; pin. Stitch around perimeter, leaving 6-inch opening for turning.

Step 8. Turn pillow right side out, insert pillow form and close opening with hand stitches.

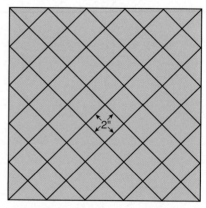

Fig. 1 Mark grid on pillow as shown.

Step 9. Make cuts in the fringe extensions with scissors. Make cuts perpendicular to pillow, ¼ inch apart. Stop cuts ¼ inch from stitching line. ■

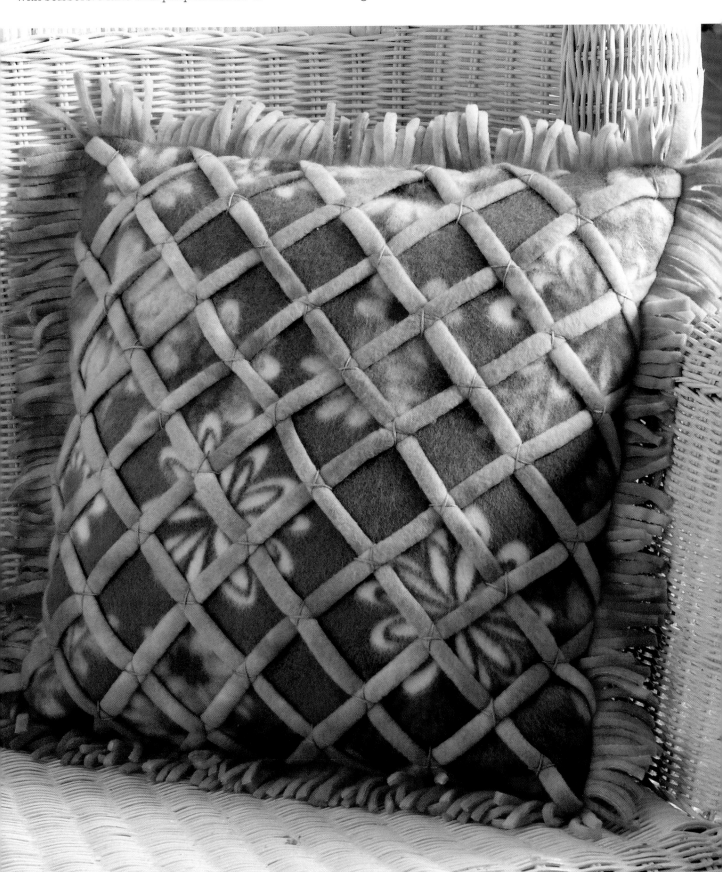

Comfy Lounge Pillow By Carol Zentgraf

Curl up in bed with this great pillow and you will read till the last page is turned!

Project Specifications
Skill Level: Beginner
Pillow Size: Varies with pattern

Materials
Designer Note: *To plan the flannel fabrics for mixing, choose one main fabric with multiple colors, such as the large plaid on the pillow front shown in the photo. Using these colors as a guide, select several other fabrics that feature these colors, varying the sizes of the plaids and checks.*

- Commercial pattern for lounge pillow
- 4 or 5 coordinating plaid or checked flannels to equal yardage recommended on pattern
- $7^1/_2$ x 12-inch plaid flannel rectangle that contrasts with fabric used for either pillow outer arm
- $11^1/_2$ x 16-inch plaid flannel rectangle that contrasts with fabric used for pillow back
- Polyester fiberfill as recommended on pattern
- All-purpose threads to match fabrics
- Basic sewing supplies and tools

Instructions
Step 1. Cut pattern pieces from fabrics using contrasting colors for adjacent pieces.

Step 2. Press under $1/2$ inch on both short edges and one long edge of $11^{1}/2$ x 16-inch back pocket rectangle. Finish the remaining long edge with serging or zigzag stitches. Press that edge under 1 inch and topstitch $3/4$ inch from the fold. This will be the upper edge of the pocket.

Step 3. Center pocket on right side of pillow back and topstitch the side and lower edges in place, stitching $1/8$ inch from edges.

Step 4. Finish one long edge of $7^{1}/2$ x 12-inch arm pocket by serging or zigzagging. Press the finished edge under 1 inch and topstitch $3/4$ inch from the fold.

Step 5. Place pocket on the right side of one outer arm piece, aligning the lower edges. Trim the rectangle side edges even with the arm piece. Baste the pocket and arm piece side and lower edges together.

Step 6. Follow the commercial pattern to finish and stuff the pillow. ■

Reversible Rug By Judith Sandstrom

Soft, cozy and washable—perfect for bed or bath.

Project Specifications
Skill Level: Beginner
Rug Size: Approximately 27 x 24 inches

Materials
- $1/4$ yard each of 8 coordinating print or solid flannels
- $1/4$ yard contrasting flannel for binding, or may use one of the flannels used in the rug
- $1^3/4$ yards cream flannel
- Craft-size thin cotton batting
- 3 rolls of $1/4$-inch quilter's iron-on adhesive tape
- Rotary-cutting tools
- Basic sewing supplies and tools

Instructions
Step 1. Prewash and iron all fabrics.

Step 2. From the cream flannel, cut twenty 3-inch strips across the width of the fabric.

Step 3. From each of the eight print or solid flannels, cut three 3-inch strips across the width of the fabric.

Step 4. From the binding flannel, cut three $2^1/2$-inch strips across the width of the fabric.

Step 5. From the cotton batting, cut 44 strips 1 x 36 inches.

Step 6. The rug is planned to have 44 woven segments. The model uses only 43 because the next color in the sequence is used for the binding. There are 24 colored segments (three of each of the eight fabrics) and 20 cream segments.

Step 7. To make each segment, place a cream or colored flannel strip right side up on ironing surface. Following manufacturer's instructions, iron a piece of $1/4$-inch quilter's iron-on adhesive tape to one long edge of fabric strip. Do not remove paper backing. Turn the strip over so the wrong side is up. Fold under the bonded edge.

Step 8. Place a batting strip $7/8$ inch from the non-bonded edge. Place the iron up and down onto the batting without gliding it. The batting will adhere to the flannel even though it is not fusible batting. Fold over the non-bonded edge of the flannel and press onto the batting. Remove the paper backing from the bonded edge. Fold over the bonded edge and iron it permanently into place to complete the segment. Repeat for all required segments. (Segments will be approximately $1^1/8$ inches wide.)

Step 9. Lay out the eight colored segments in a pleasing order with the overlapped edges on the bottom. Repeat the sequence three times. Carefully weave the cream segments over and under the colored segments. Push the segments closely together in order to maintain straight squared edges.

Step 10. When weaving is complete, even the ends of the segments by trimming away the excess fabric.

Step 11. Place each of the binding strips right side up on the ironing surface. Iron a piece of 1/4-inch quilter's tape to both long edges of each strip. Press under the bonded edges and press the strip in half. Remove the paper backing on only one edge of each strip.

Step 12. With right sides together, place the folded edge of one binding strip, with the paper backing removed, along the top side of one rug edge. The pressed line indicating the half-way mark of the strip should be at the edge of the woven rug. When the binding is perfectly aligned, iron it to the rug top. Fold the binding over to the wrong side of the rug, remove the remaining paper backing and iron the binding into place. Trim binding ends even with the rug ends. Repeat for the opposite edge of the rug.

Step 13. Follow the binding directions for the two remaining opposite edges with the exception of the binding ends. Instead of cutting them off even with the rug ends, extend them 3/8 inch beyond the rug ends. Iron a piece of 1/4-inch quilter's tape to each binding end, fold under the edges, remove the paper backing and finish ironing the binding onto the rug to properly finish the ends. ▪

Woodsie Pines Window Set

By Patsy Moreland

You don't have to have a cabin in the woods to enjoy North Woods ambience in your home!

Project Specifications
Skill Level: Beginner
Panel Size: 30 x 65 inches each
Valance Size: 16 x 71 inches
Designer Note: *Sizes may be easily altered.*

Materials
For Panels
- 2 yards green plaid flannel
- 3³/₄ yards pine-bough-print flannel
- 1 package dark green McCall's Qwik-Tach Tape
- 1 package dark green McCall's Flex-On Loops
- 1 (1-inch) dowel rod the width of window

For Valance
- 1 yard pine-bough-print flannel
- 1 yard green plaid flannel
- 1 yard lightweight or mid-weight fusible nonwoven interfacing
- Press cloth
- 1 grommet kit including at least 12 (1-inch) grommets and installation tools
- Wooden mallet
- Ball peen hammer
- Solid work surface
- ³/₈-inch metal rod the width of window

For Both
- All-purpose threads to match fabrics
- Rotary-cutting tools
- Basic sewing supplies and tools

Instructions
Note: *All seam allowances are ¹/₂ inch.*

PANELS

Step 1. Wash, dry and press all fabrics without steam. Remove selvages from fabrics. Measure and cut fabrics on the length of the fabric, not across the width.

Step 2. From pine-bough-print flannel, cut two A pieces 25 x 66 inches. From green plaid flannel, cut two B pieces 9 x 66 inches and two C pieces 5 x 66 inches.

Step 3. Pin one B strip to the left edge of one A rectangle, right sides facing; stitch. Iron the seam allowance toward the B strip.

Step 4. Turn remaining long edge of B strip under ¹/₂ inch; press. Fold the strip in half lengthwise, wrong sides facing. Turn to backside and pin along the seam stitching line. Topstitch ¹/₄ inch from folded edge.

Step 5. Pin one C strip to the other side of the A rectangle; stitch. Press seam allowance toward the A strip.

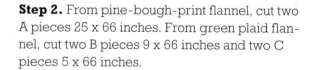

Step 6. Turn remaining long edge of A strip under $1/2$ inch; press. Fold the strip in half lengthwise, wrong sides facing. Turn to backside and pin along the seam stitching line. Topstitch $1/4$ inch from folded edge.

Step 7. Measure the width of the panel. Measure and cut the Quik-Tach Tape the same length plus 1 inch at each end. The 1-inch cut will be between two holes at each end. Remove 1 inch of the stitches at both ends, tops and lower edges of tape. Carefully cut back $1/2$ inch of the interfacing in the tape. Turn the raw edges at the end inside $1/2$ inch; steam-press and pin. Insert the top of the curtain panel raw edges between the bottom folded edges of the tape; pin.

Step 8. Begin topstitching 1 inch from the end and $1/4$ inch from the folded edge at the top, down the side, across the bottom and up the other side of the tape and at the top 1 inch in from the edge.

Step 9. The points on the plastic loops are inserted in the punched holes on the right side and the locking loops are snapped onto the points from the wrong side of the panel. Do not iron over the plastic rings.

Step 10. For hem, measure 64 inches from inside the plastic ring at the top to the bottom of the panel. Mark with a pin. Repeat six times across the bottom of the panel. Cut off any extra fabric. Turn $1/2$ inch to the wrong side twice; pin. Topstitch $1/4$ inch from folded edge.

Step 11. Repeat for second panel, but reverse the placement of B and C strips. Place the B strip on the right side of A and the C strip on the left.

Step 12. Thread the dowel rod through the rings and hang.

VALANCE

Step 1. Wash, dry and press all fabrics without steam. Remove selvages from fabrics. Measure and cut fabrics on the width of the fabric.

Step 2. From pine-bough-print flannel, cut two A pieces $13 1/2$ x 37 inches. Join two pieces on one short end, wrong sides facing. Press seams together. Sew the same seam, right sides facing, to enclose the seam allowance

Step 3. Turn $1/2$ inch to the wrong side twice at each short end; pin. Topstitch $1/8$ inch from folded edge.

Step 4. Turn 1 inch to the wrong side twice on one long edge; pin. Topstitch $1/4$ inch from folded edge.

Step 5. From green plaid flannel, cut two B pieces $10 1/2$ x 37 inches. Join pieces and hem short edges as in Steps 2 and 3 above; hem both long edges as in Step 4.

Step 6. Fold the B strip in half lengthwise, wrong sides facing; press.

Step 7. Cut two strips of fusible interfacing 4 x 36 inches. Butt the strips end to end on the wrong side of half of the B strip. Fuse according to manufacturer's instructions.

Step 8. Place the right side of the unhemmed edge of the A strip over the wrong-side hem of B. Fold the top half wrong side over B and topstitch all edges $1/8$ inch from edge. Topstitch two rows $1/4$ inch apart where A and B are inserted.

Step 9. Measure the width of B and mark at half the width. Measure and mark $1 1/2$ inches from each end of B.

Step 10. Put grommets in the fabric header at the marked $1 1/2$-inch marks according to manufacturer's instructions. Space the remaining 10 grommets in increments of 6 inches. ■

Flannel Message Center

By Carla G. Schwab

This little wall quilt is planned to accept pinned-on notes and reminders for family communication.

Project Specifications
Skill Level: Beginner
Message Center Size: 14 x 24 inches

Materials
- Plaid flannel $10^1/_2$ x $9^1/_2$ inches
- $^1/_2$ yard gold checked flannel
- $^1/_2$ yard dark red floral flannel for borders
- Flannel backing 18 x 28 inches
- Thin batting 18 x 28 inches
- Scrap of cream fleece for pitcher
- 2 yards red single-fold binding
- Two stems of silk flowers to insert in pitcher
- All-purpose threads to match fabrics
- Basic sewing supplies and tools

Instructions
Step 1. From gold checked flannel, cut one rectangle $10^1/_2$ x $11^1/_2$ inches.

Step 2. From white fleece, cut pitcher and pitcher liner for appliqué. Referring to photo, position pitcher along lower edge of gold checked flannel rectangle. Hand- or machine-appliqué pitcher liner and pitcher, leaving pitcher open at top for insertion of flowers.

Step 3. Sew plaid flannel rectangle to gold checked rectangle along the $10^1/_2$-inch edge, catching the lower edge of the pitcher in the seam.

Step 4. Baste the red single-fold binding along the edges of the assembled pieces.

Step 5. From dark red floral flannel, cut two strips each $2^1/_2$ x 15 inches and $2^1/_2$ x 25 inches. With right sides facing, sew borders to background, mitering corners. Trim to square and press.

Step 6. Layer backing, batting and quilt top; baste or pin. Quilt around the pitcher, along the seam line between rectangles and along the seam line of the border. Trim batting and backing even with top.

Step 7. Cut and connect $2^1/_2$-inch strips of gold checked flannel to make $2^1/_2$ yards of binding. Bind message center to finish.

Step 8. Insert silk flowers in pitcher, trimming stems if needed. ■

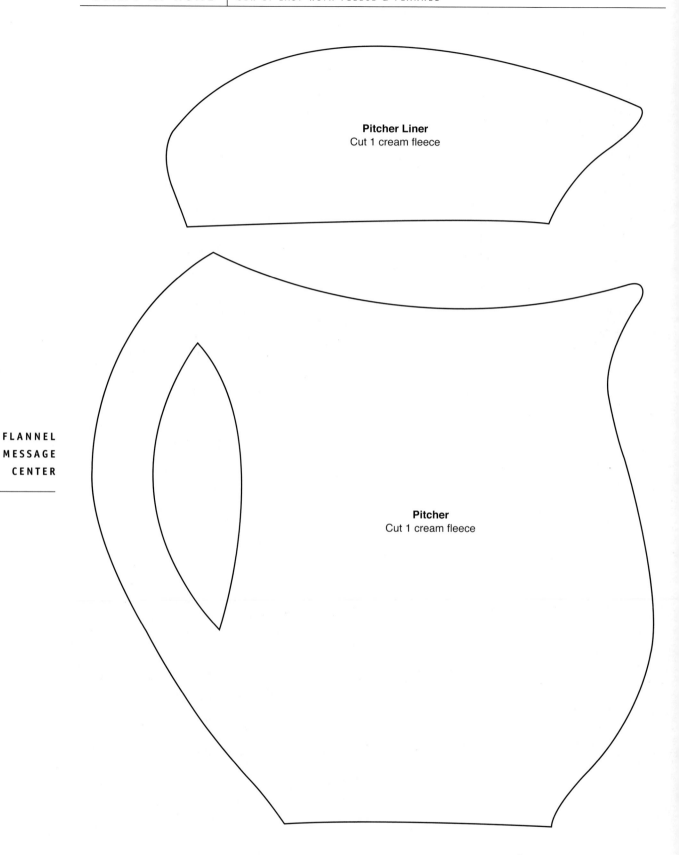

Pitcher Liner
Cut 1 cream fleece

**FLANNEL
MESSAGE
CENTER**

Pitcher
Cut 1 cream fleece

Snowflake Winter Warmer

By Carol Zentgraf

A reverse-appliqué effect is so easy to achieve with fleece!

Project Specifications
Skill Level: Beginner
Scarf Size: Approximately 10^1/$_2$ x 62 inches
Hat Size: Any size

Materials
- Commercial lined hat pattern with turned-up brim (Kwik Sew pattern 2891 used for model)
- Fleece yardage as recommended on pattern
- 1 rectangle in each of 2 hat fleece colors 10^1/$_2$ x 62 inches
- Tracing paper
- Quilting thread to match darker fleece
- All-purpose thread to match darker fleece
- Small, sharp-pointed scissors
- Quilt basting spray
- Rotary-cutting tools, optional
- Basic sewing supplies and tools

Instructions

SCARF

Step 1. Layer the two 10^1/$_2$ x 62-inch rectangles wrong sides facing and raw edges even. Using a ^{1}/$_4$-inch seam allowance, sew the long edges together to within 5 inches of each end. Sew across the layers 5 inches from each end.

Step 2. Trace the snowflake pattern onto tracing paper four times and cut out. Lightly spray each snowflake with quilt basting spray. Refer to the photo for placement and adhere two snowflakes to each end of the scarf on the darker fleece side. Place the lower snowflake approximately 1^1/$_2$ inches above the crosswise stitching at each end.

Step 3. With quilting thread in the needle and all-purpose thread in the bobbin, stitch around each snowflake on the darker fleece side, ^{1}/$_8$ inch from the edge.

Step 4. Remove the pattern pieces. Carefully cutting through the darker fleece layer only, cut out each snowflake ^{1}/$_8$ inch inside the stitching line.

Step 5. At each end of scarf, cut the fleece into ^{1}/$_2$-inch-wide fringe strips perpendicular to the crosswise stitching line. Stop cuts ^{1}/$_4$ inch from stitching line.

HAT

Step 1. Follow pattern directions to cut and sew hat, using the darker fleece color as the contrasting folded-up brim.

Step 2. Cut the ends off one previously used snowflake as indicated on pattern. Spray lightly with basting spray if no longer sticky enough to adhere. Stitch and cut as in Steps 3 and 4. ∎

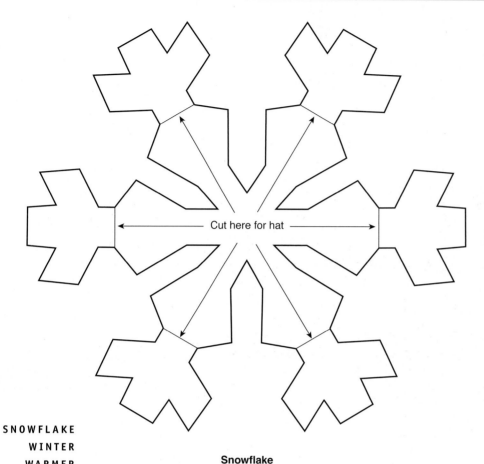

Snowflake

SNOWFLAKE
WINTER
WARMER

Front view of cut-out snowflake.

Back view of stitched snowflake.

SHIMMERING
STRANDS
KIMONO

Shimmering Strands Kimono
Continued from page 84

cut off 1³/₈ inches from the hemline. Cut two 5-inch-wide bands the same length as the bottom width of the sleeve.

Step 6. Cut fronts, back and sleeves from the lining fabric. Construct the jacket front, back and sleeves of the embellished flannel and lining. Do not sew the bands on. Hem the bottom of both the kimono and lining. Turn the fabrics right side out; place the lining shell inside the jacket.

Step 7. Baste the lining to the kimono along the front, neckline and sleeves. Follow the pattern directions to sew the front band to the kimono. Sew the sleeve bands in the same manner.

Step 8. Cut the sash pieces from contrasting flannel. Follow the pattern directions to sew the sash. ■

CUDDLE ME BABY

The fleece and flannel of today is so easy to sew and so soft that it is the ideal fabric to use for babies.

Ready for Travel By Holly Daniels

Patterns and instructions for both of these adorable jacket and hat sets are included in this project.

Project Specifications
Skill Level: Beginner
Jacket Size: Toddler
Hat Size: Toddler

Materials
Pink Set
- $1/2$ yard pink fleece
- 3 yards pastel decorative trim
- 4 ($1/2$-inch) buttons)
- 1 large snap for bonnet
- 4 large snaps for jacket, optional
- 2 strips fusible interfacing 1 x 11 inches

Blue Set
- $1/2$ yard blue fleece
- 3 $1/2$ yards narrow fold-over binding
- 5 ($5/8$-inch) buttons
- 2 strips fusible interfacing 1 x 11 inches
- 5 large snaps for jacket, optional

Both Sets
- All-purpose threads to match fabrics
- Pattern paper
- Basic sewing supplies and tools

Instructions
Designer Notes: Seam allowances are $1/2$ inch unless otherwise noted. Machine buttonholes through layers of fleece are somewhat difficult. Either work buttonholes by hand or substitute large snaps for the actual closures with decorative buttons sewn to the outside.

PINK JACKET

Step 1. Following the instructions in **Fig. 1**, draw and cut out patterns for jacket front, back and sleeve from pattern paper, cutting away gray-shaded areas. Place on pink fleece and cut out.

Step 2. Mark fronts, back and sleeves by basting along 3-inch lines as designated on patterns.

Step 3. Sew fronts and back together at shoulder seams.

Step 4. Fold sleeves lengthwise to find center point. Match center point to shoulder seam and stitch.

Step 5. Fold raw edge of fabric up to basted line on outside of sleeve as shown in **Fig. 2**. Stitch in place $1/8$ inch from raw edge.

Step 6. Cut $1/4$-inch fringe through both layers perpendicular to seam as shown in **Fig. 3**. Do not cut through the loop at bottom. Repeat Steps 5 and 6 for second sleeve.

Step 7. Cut two pieces of pastel decorative trim the width of a sleeve. Center over stitched lines, covering the raw edges of turned-up hems. Sew to sleeves, securing both long edges of the trim.

Step 8. Sew side seam from the top of the fringe on each sleeve to the basted lines on the jacket. Leave the bottom of the seams open below the basted lines. Clip and trim the underarm seams as needed so seams will lie flat. Secure ends of trim at sleeve edges by hand.

Step 9. Baste one strip of 1 x 11-inch fusible interfacing to wrong side of each jacket front facing. Machine-zigzag to secure raw edges. Fold the facings to the inside of the jacket to enclose the interfacing. Topstitch 1 inch from the folded front edge.

Step 10. Make fringe at the bottom edge of the jacket as in sleeves, Steps 5 and 6.

Step 11. Cut one piece of pastel decorative trim the length of the fringed area plus 2 inches. Sew over stitched line, leaving 1 inch extending over fold at front of jacket. Fold the extended piece back into the jacket and secure inside with hand stitches.

Step 12. Fold the raw edge of the neck down 1/4 inch and baste. Cut one piece of pastel decorative trim the length of the neckline plus 2 inches. Apply pastel decorative trim over basting, allowing 1 inch of trim to extend past the center folds. Secure the extended ends to the inside of the jacket with hand stitches.

Step 13. For girl's jacket, lap the right side over the left. Make four buttonholes in top flap and sew four buttons to bottom, or sew four snaps to inside flaps and sew four decorative buttons over the snaps.

PINK BONNET

Step 1. Cut one piece of pink fleece 8 x 14 inches. Mark and baste a line 3 inches from one long raw edge. Make fringed edge as in Jacket Steps 5 and 6.

Step 2. Cut two pieces of pastel decorative trim the length of the fringed edge plus 2 inches. Sew one strip to fringe as in Jacket Step 11. Sew second strip of trim 1 inch from first.

Step 3. Cut one piece of pink fleece 4 x 6 1/2 inches for bonnet back. Round both corners on one short side as shown in **Fig. 4**. Fold both the fringed bonnet strip and the bonnet back in half to find center backs; pin. Pin remaining edges of bonnet back to bonnet strip; sew.

READY FOR
TRAVEL

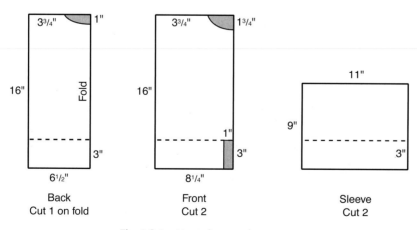

Fig. 1 Cut pattern pieces as shown.

Fig. 2 Fold end of sleeve up as shown and sew.

Step 4. Cut one piece of pink fleece 1 x 5 inches for neck strap. Fold strip in half lengthwise and sew to form strap. Stitch one end to bonnet inside front. Sew a snap to the other end and to inside edge of other bonnet side.

BLUE JACKET

Step 1. Follow Pink Jacket Step 1 instructions for patterns and cutting, except make the lower edge of jacket fronts and back on what was the previous 3-inch basting line. Sleeves should be cut 5 x 11 inches. Place on blue fleece and cut out.

Step 2. Sew fronts and back together at shoulder seams.

Step 3. Cut two pieces of narrow fold-over binding the width of each sleeve. Sew to wrist edge of each sleeve.

Step 4. Sew side seam from wrist edge to jacket lower edge. Clip and trim seam as needed under arms. Secure edges of binding at inner wrists.

Step 5. Cut one piece of narrow fold-over binding the length of lower jacket edge, including interfaced area. Sew trim to edge of jacket.

Step 6. Cut one piece of narrow fold-over binding the length of neckline, including the facing area. Sew to neckline.

Step 7. Apply fusible interfacing strips as in Pink Jacket, Step 9.

Step 8. Secure trimmed neck and hem edges with hand stitches.

Step 9. Attach five fasteners to front of jacket as in Pink Jacket, Step 13. Lap left side over right if boy's jacket.

BLUE BONNET

Step 1. Cut one piece of blue fleece 6 x 14 inches. Round both corners of one long edge as shown in **Fig. 5**.

Step 2. Cut one piece of blue fleece 4 x 6 inches. Curve corners and attach to bonnet strip as in Pink Bonnet, Step 3.

Step 3. Apply narrow fold-over binding to all raw edges of bonnet, beginning and ending at back neck edge.

Step 4. Cut two 8-inch pieces of narrow fold-over binding for ties. Sew folded edges together to secure. Sew one end to the inside edge, each side of bonnet. ▪

Fig. 3 Cut fringe as shown.

Fig. 4 Round corners of bonnet back as shown.

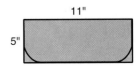

Fig. 5 Round corners of bonnet strip as shown.

Kid's Kimono By June Fiechter

A bright bit of style for any little girl— yet soft and cuddly and warm.

Project Specifications

Skill Level: Beginner
Jacket Size: Any size

Materials

- Commercial jacket pattern (New Look pattern #6880 used for model)
- Royal blue wool flannel in amount recommended by pattern
- Yellow flannel for lining in amount recommended by pattern plus scraps for appliqué
- Wool scraps in shades of orange, blue and green
- All-purpose threads to match fabrics
- Fabric glue
- Basic sewing supplies and tools

Instructions

Step 1. Follow instructions on pattern to cut out jacket and lining.

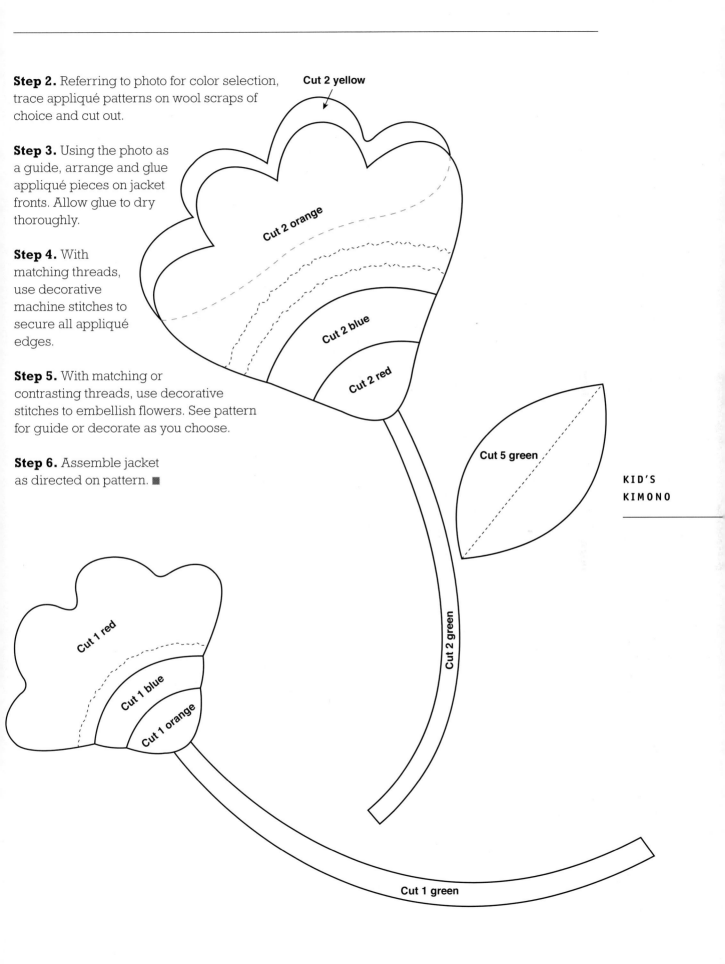

Step 2. Referring to photo for color selection, trace appliqué patterns on wool scraps of choice and cut out.

Step 3. Using the photo as a guide, arrange and glue appliqué pieces on jacket fronts. Allow glue to dry thoroughly.

Step 4. With matching threads, use decorative machine stitches to secure all appliqué edges.

Step 5. With matching or contrasting threads, use decorative stitches to embellish flowers. See pattern for guide or decorate as you choose.

Step 6. Assemble jacket as directed on pattern. ▦

Cut 2 yellow

Cut 2 orange

Cut 2 blue

Cut 2 red

Cut 5 green

Cut 2 green

Cut 1 red

Cut 1 blue

Cut 1 orange

Cut 1 green

KID'S KIMONO

Baby Jacket Fun
By Carol Zentgraf

Even babies like variety, and the closure designs of this jacket could be endless!

Project Specifications
Skill Level: Beginner
Jacket Size: Any size

Materials
- Commercial pattern designed for fleece (Kwik Sew pattern #3127 used for model)
- Pink fleece in yardage recommended on pattern
- 2 yellow print scraps 4 inches square
- 2 pink print scraps 4 inches square
- 2 heavy-duty fusible web 4-inch squares
- 4 (1-inch) hook-and-loop dots
- 2-inch piece of pink Chenille by the Inch
- 4-inch piece of yellow Chenille by the Inch
- Chenille brush
- Spray bottle of water
- Rotary-cutting tools
- Permanent fabric glue
- Basic sewing supplies and tools

Instructions
Step 1. Follow pattern instructions to cut out and sew baby jacket. Use two hook-and-loop dots for front closure.

Step 2. Topstitch front overlap 1¹/₄ inches from edge and lower edge of jacket and sleeves ³/₄ inch from edge.

Step 3. Trace flower pattern on paper side of fusible web as instructed on pattern. Cut out, leaving roughly ¹/₄-inch margin around traced lines.

Step 4. Following manufacturer's instructions, fuse to one pink print fabric square. Cut out on traced lines. Remove paper backing and fuse to wrong side of other pink print fabric square. Cut out along original outline to make flower shape with fabric on both sides.

Step 5. Cut a ¹/₂-inch strip of yellow Chenille by the Inch and stitch to center of flower. Sew a yellow strip around the center, trimming any excess. Spray with water and brush with chenille brush, protecting the fabric flower with paper. Allow to dry thoroughly.

Step 6. Use permanent fabric glue to adhere soft portion of hook-and-loop dot to front of jacket, 2¹/₄ inches from neckline. Glue hook portion of dot to back of flower.

Step 7. Repeat Steps 3 and 4 with butterfly design.

Step 8. Sew pink Chenille by the Inch to center of butterfly, trimming as necessary. Spray, brush and dry as in Step 5.

Step 9. Glue hook portion of remaining hook-and-loop dot to back of butterfly. Butterfly and flower may be interchanged as well as any other designs you may choose to make. ■

Drawings continued on page 132

Polar Pal Jacket

By Willow Ann Sirch

Polar bears that inhabit arctic regions
love the warmth of flannel, too.

Project Specifications
Skill Level: Beginner
Jacket Size: 18–24 months

Materials
- Scraps of white flannel
- $1/4$ yard dark blue mottled flannel
- $1/2$ yard each blue print and beige calico flannel
- 2 ($3/4$-inch) hook-and-loop dots
- All-purpose threads to match fabrics
- Black 6-strand embroidery floss
- Embroidery needle
- Small amount of polyester fiberfill
- Quilting thread
- Rotary-cutting tools
- Basic sewing supplies and tools

Instructions
Step 1. Trace and cut polar bear pocket toy as instructed on pattern, adding $3/16$-inch seam allowance. Trace and cut polar bear appliqué as instructed on pattern, adding $1/4$-inch seam allowance.

Step 2. Turn under the seam allowance on polar bear appliqué and baste in place. With 6 strands of black embroidery floss, embroider eyes, nose and mouth.

Step 3. With 6 strands of black embroidery floss, embroider eyes, nose and mouth on right side of one polar bear toy. Place both pieces of polar bear toy together, right sides facing. Stitch around perimeter, leaving $1^{1}/2$ inches unsewn for turning and stuffing. Turn right side out, stuff lightly with polyester fiberfill and close opening with hand stitches.

Step 4. On blue print flannel, lay out and mark two sleeves, one back and two jacket fronts (flip pattern for second front). Repeat from beige calico flannel for lining. Cut out pieces, adding $5/8$-inch seam allowance.

Step 5. Stitch jacket fronts to back at shoulders. Press seams open. Fold and press sleeves lengthwise to mark exact center of each sleeve shoulder. With right sides facing, pin and sew each sleeve shoulder to the jacket front/back piece. Press seams open.

Step 6. Construct jacket lining same as jacket, Step 5.

Step 7. Jacket right sides facing, pin and stitch from wrist to, but not into, underarm. Sew down jacket side. Repeat for second sleeve. Press seams open. Repeat for lining.

Step 8. Center polar bear appliqué on blue jacket back. Appliqué in place by hand or machine.

Step 9. Cut pocket from dark blue mottled flannel 4³/₄ x 5¹/₄ inches. Turn under pocket top once and then again. Stitch ¹/₄ inch inside the top edge of the pocket.

Step 10. Fold remaining pocket edges under ¹/₄ inch; press. Position on jacket right front as shown in photo. Machine-stitch in place.

Step 11. Wrong sides facing, position jacket lining inside blue jacket. Trim any excess fabric so that jacket and lining align all the way around the outside of the jacket and at the ends of each sleeve.

Step 12. Quilt ¹/₄ inch from the outer edge of the polar bear appliqué. Trace the polar bear quilting pattern on the left jacket front and quilt on traced lines.

Step 13. Pin and machine-baste edges of jacket and lining together, starting at the base of one side of jacket front opening, around the collar, down the other side of jacket opening, around the lower edge and coming back to the front.

Step 14. From dark blue mottled fabric, cut three 2¹/₄-inch-wide strips across the width of the fabric for binding. Fold each strip in half lengthwise, wrong sides facing; press.

Step 15. Align raw edges of binding with raw edges of jacket. Machine-stitch with ¹/₄-inch seam allowance. Flip binding over its own raw edge and pin fold of binding to lining of jacket. About ³/₈ inch of binding should show on jacket and lining sides. Hand-stitch to lining. Cover the raw edge of the end of each binding strip with the folded edge of the next strip.

Step 16. Sew hook-and-loop dots to jacket fronts for closure.

Step 17. Insert polar bear toy in jacket pocket. ■

POLAR PAL JACKET

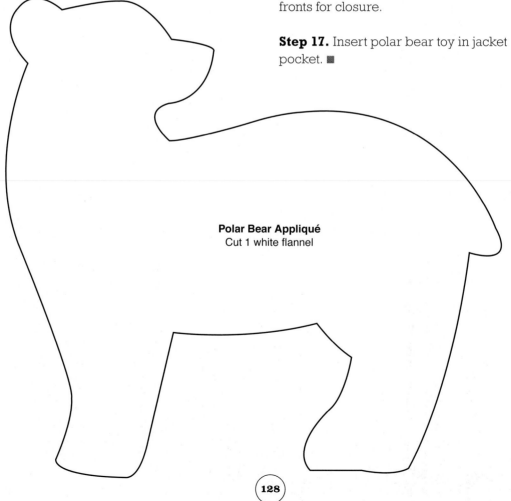

Polar Bear Appliqué
Cut 1 white flannel

Jacket Sleeve
Cut 2 blue print & 2 beige calico
Enlarge pattern 133% before cutting

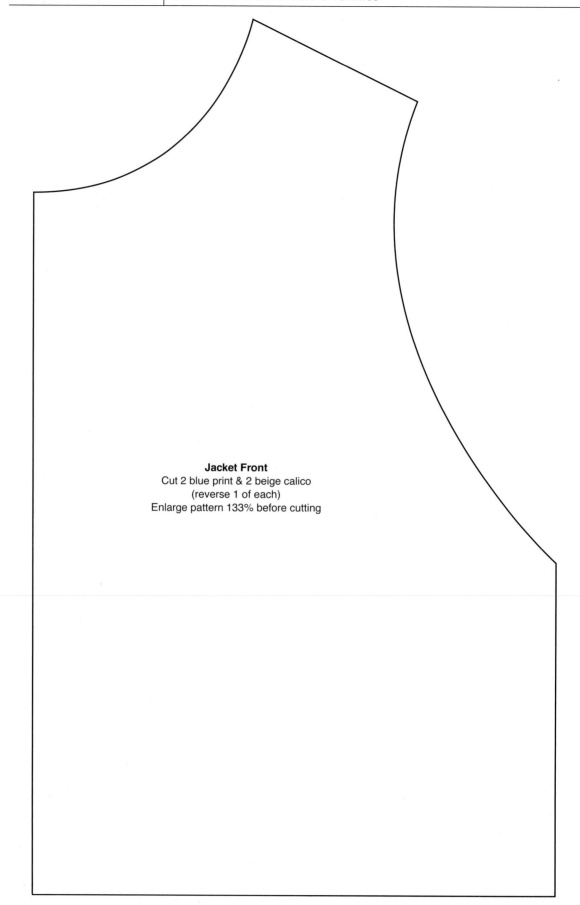

Jacket Front
Cut 2 blue print & 2 beige calico
(reverse 1 of each)
Enlarge pattern 133% before cutting

Jacket Back
Cut 1 blue print & 1 beige calico
Enlarge pattern 133% before cutting

Place line on fold

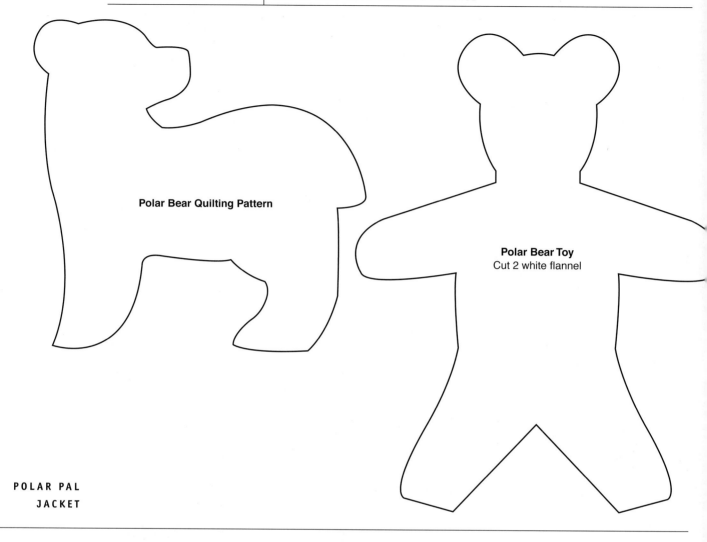

Polar Bear Quilting Pattern

Polar Bear Toy
Cut 2 white flannel

**POLAR PAL
JACKET**

**BABY
JACKET
FUN**

Baby Jacket Fun
Continued from page 125

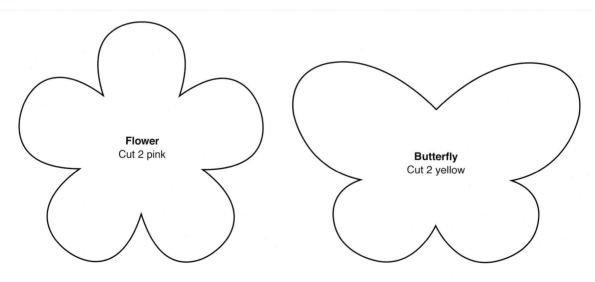

Flower
Cut 2 pink

Butterfly
Cut 2 yellow

From Bag to Pad By Bev Shenefield

This dual-duty item will be loved by anyone

transporting an infant!

Project Specifications
Skill Level: Beginner
Bag Size: Approximately 18 x 12 inches closed
  and 18 x 30 inches open

Materials
- $1^1/_2$ yards navy solid flannel
- $1^1/_2$ yards teddy bear plaid flannel
- 3 yards thin cotton batting
- Navy buttonhole thread
- Navy all-purpose thread
- 2 ($1^3/_8$-inch) red buttons
- 1 yard $^3/_4$-inch-wide navy hook-and-loop tape
- Pattern paper
- Basic sewing supplies and tools

Instructions
Step 1. Cut two flap pieces and one $30^1/_4$ x $17^1/_2$-inch rectangle from pattern paper. Lay flap pieces along opposite sides of rectangle $7^1/_4$ inches from the end as shown in **Fig. 1**. Tape pieces together to create bag/pad pattern.

Step 2. Use pattern created in Step 1 to cut one navy flannel and two thin batting pieces. Mark fold lines on navy flannel piece.

Step 3. Place navy flannel bag/pad on work surface, right side down. Place batting bag/pad (2 layers) on flannel and pin in place.

Step 4. Cut a piece of teddy bear plaid flannel 43 x 36 inches. Be sure the lines of plaid run straight in both directions. Place on top of

pinned navy flannel and batting. Remove previous pins and pin all layers together, making certain all layers are smooth and have no creases.

Step 5. Following the lines on the plaid flannel, stitch both vertically and horizontally to form quilted squares. Start sewing across the narrow width, starting in the center and working out to each end. Repeat with length.

Step 6. For strap, cut one strip of thin cotton batting $2^1/_4$ x 42 inches and one strip of teddy bear plaid 6 x 43 inches. Center the batting strip on the wrong side of the teddy bear strip. Fold each side of flannel strip to back of strip, turning under one raw edge. Sew down the center of the strip. Fold ends in $^1/_4$ inch and stitch.

Step 7. Trim teddy bear plaid around bag on flat sides $1^1/_2$ inches from the pattern edges. Leave $^3/_8$ inch on the rounded flap ends. Turn under the edges on the straight sides of bag, then turn under again; bring folded edge to lining side of bag and stitch in place by machine.

Step 8. Turn flap edges to inside and hand-stitch in place. From teddy bear plaid, cut two strips $1^1/_4$ x 26 inches. Fold under one long edge of each strip; press.

Step 9. Pin folded edge of strip along edge of rounded flaps on lining side of pad. Machine-stitch in place. Turn

under the other long edge and stitch in place to enclose all raw edges.

Step 10. Fold lower edge of bag up on fold line. Fold upper edge down over lower edge. Fold flaps on fold lines to create a gusset for bag sides. Mark overlap and stitch hook-and-loop tape in place for closure. Sew soft side of tape to lining side of bag and loop side to plaid side.

Step 11. Sew 1-inch strips of hook-and-loop tape at intervals around the flap edges to hold gusset securely in position when used as a bag.

Step 12. Sew red buttons to flaps as indicated on pattern. Enclose one end of strap between one button and flap and stitch securely. On the other side, work two buttonholes, one in the strap and one in the overlap of the bag. Button will go through both buttonholes. ◼

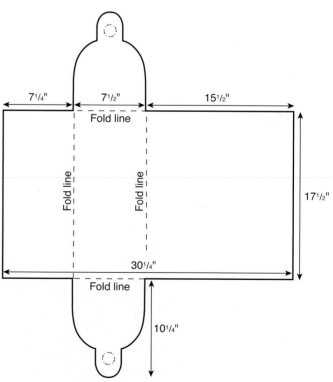

Fig. 1 Make pattern as shown.

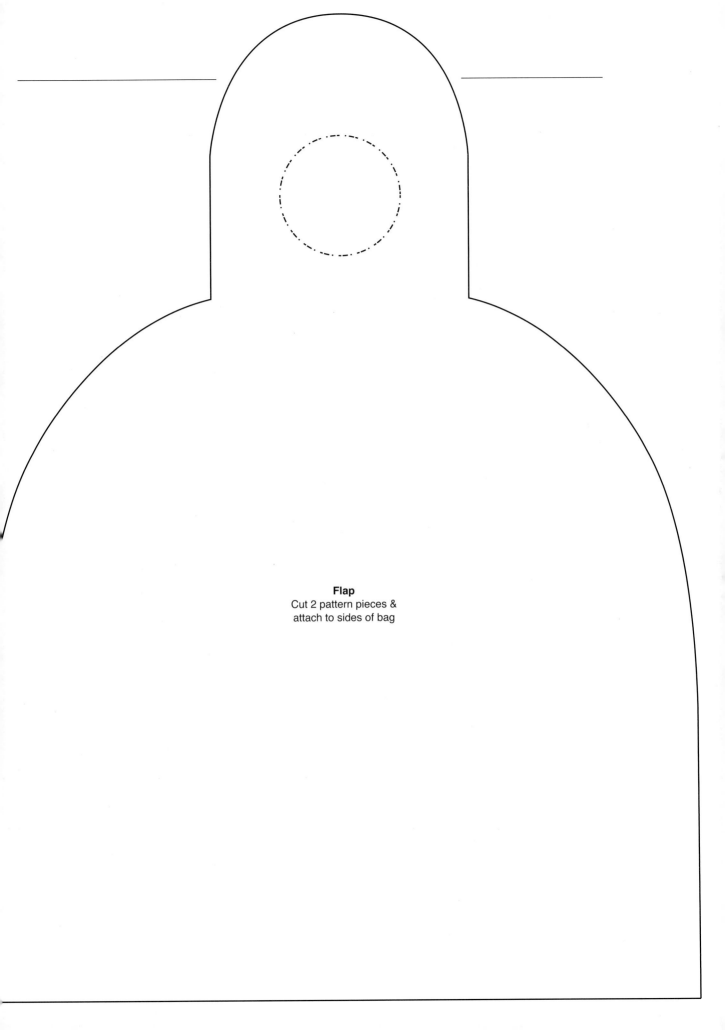

Flap
Cut 2 pattern pieces &
attach to sides of bag

Flower Bright Jumper & Hat

By Chris Malone

Sunshine bright and happy for a spunky little girl!

Project Specifications
Skill Level: Beginner
Jumper Size: Baby Small–Large

Materials
- Commercial pattern for pinafore/jumper, panties and hat with brim (Simplicity #9784, views B, CC and E used for model)
- Small pieces of yellow, green and a second coordinating solid-color flannel
- $1/4$ yard coordinating solid-color flannel for pocket and two flowers
- Approximately 1 yard each of two coordinating flannel prints. Check yardage requirements for pattern and size
- $3/8$ yard lightweight fusible interfacing
- 1 package $1/4$-inch-wide elastic
- All-purpose threads to match fabrics
- $5/8$ yard of $5/8$-inch-wide grosgrain ribbon for inside of hat band
- $7/8$ yard of $3/8$-inch-wide grosgrain ribbon for hat ties
- 4 ($7/8$-inch) any-color shank buttons for flower centers
- 2 ($5/8$-inch) buttons to match jumper
- Washable fabric glue, optional
- Basic sewing supplies and tools

Instructions
Step 1. Cut jumper, including bodice lining, from one flannel print. Cut panties and hat from second flannel print. See Step 3 for pocket cutting and sewing instructions. Cut interfacing according to pattern instructions.

Step 2. Construct jumper, panties and hat following pattern instructions. Finish any exposed seams by serging or pinking.

Step 3. To make a self-lined pocket, cut a 5 x 9-inch rectangle from flannel. Fold the pocket in half crosswise, right sides facing, and sew edges with a $1/2$-inch seam, leaving an opening along one edge for turning. Trim the corners and grade seam allowance. Turn right side out and press. Close opening with hand stitches. With matching thread, topstitch all around pocket $3/8$ inch from the edge. Pin pocket to one side of jumper front and stitch sides and bottom $1/8$ inch from edge.

Step 4. Trace 24 flower petals on non-adhesive side of interfacing. Trace the leaf five times. Cut out on traced lines. Following the manufacturer's instructions, fuse 12 petals each to two different solid-colored flannels. Fuse leaves to green flannel. Leave at least $3/8$ inch between shapes.

Step 5. Fold flannel, right sides facing, with interfacing shapes on top as shown in **Fig. 1**. Sew around each traced petal with the needle directly beside the edge of the interfacing. Do not stitch across the flat end. Cut out $1/8$ inch from seam; clip curves and turn right side out.

Step 6. For leaves, sew as for petals but sew side seams ¹/₄ inch longer than bottom of interfacing leaf as shown in **Fig. 2**. Cut out and turn as for petals.

Step 7. Turn bottom edge of leaves in ¹/₄ inch and close the opening with hand stitches. Knot the thread but do not clip. Fold a pleat in the center of each leaf at the bottom and tack with thread. Repeat for five leaves.

Step 8. Hand-sew a running stitch along the bottom edge of each petal with doubled matching thread; pull to gather. With the same thread, add a second petal and gather. Repeat until six petals are joined. Attach the last petal to the first petal to form a circle. Pull thread to gather petals tightly and knot. Do not cut thread. Leave thread hanging loose to attach flower to clothing.

Step 9. Cut four flower centers from yellow flannel. With doubled matching thread, hand-sew a running stitch all around the edge of the fabric circle ¹/₈ inch from the edge.

Step 10. Place the rounded side of a shank button in the center of a fabric circle on the wrong side. Pull the thread to bring the fabric up and around the shank. Knot the thread but do not clip. Slip the needle through the fabric so it comes out at the side edge of the button. Place the button in the center of a flower and slipstitch the edges of the center to the petals. If desired, washable fabric glue may be used to hold the center in place.

Step 11. Tack two matching flowers to the bodice front, over the straps. Sew one flower to top of pocket, being careful not to sew through to the jumper skirt. Tuck two leaves under petals and slipstitch in place.

Step 12. Pull hat brim up on one side and tack in place with a few stitches. Tack one flower and three leaves to the underside of the brim as shown in photo. ■

FLOWER
BRIGHT
JUMPER &
HAT

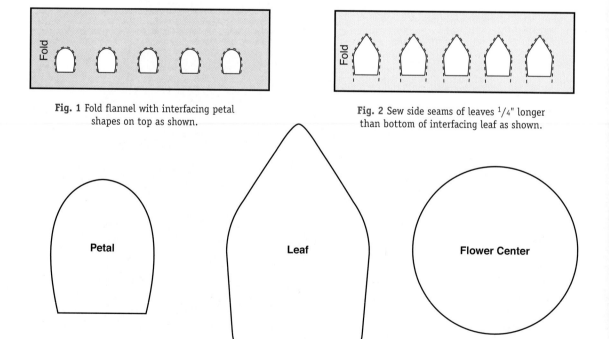

Fold

Fig. 1 Fold flannel with interfacing petal shapes on top as shown.

Fold

Fig. 2 Sew side seams of leaves ¹/₄" longer than bottom of interfacing leaf as shown.

Petal

Leaf

Flower Center

Nightie Night Giraffe Sleeper

By June Fiechter

This bright giraffe will bring a smile to everyone's face!

Project Specifications
Skill Level: Beginner
Sleeper Size: Newborn–18 months

Materials

- Commercial sleeper pattern with hood (Simplicity pattern #5749 used for model)
- Scraps of brown flannel for appliqué
- Light blue fleece as recommended on pattern
- ¼ yard yellow solid flannel for giraffe
- ¼ yard green solid flannel for hood lining and giraffe spots
- All-purpose threads to match fabrics
- Brown 6-strand embroidery floss
- ½-inch hook-and-loop dot
- 12-inch zipper
- 1 package ¼-inch-wide elastic
- Fabric glue
- Basic sewing supplies and tools

Instructions
Step 1. Cut out pattern pieces according to pattern directions from blue fleece. Cut hood lining from green flannel.

Step 2. Sew seam down front of sleeper and sew in zipper.

Step 3. Place sleeper front on work surface.

Step 4. Use pattern provided to cut out giraffe from yellow flannel. Cut spots from green flannel and nose and hoofs from brown flannel scraps.

Step 5. Using photo and pattern as a guide, glue pieces to front of sleeper. With matching thread and satin stitch or buttonhole stitch, machine-stitch around all appliqué pieces.

Step 6. With 2 strands of brown embroidery floss, make two French knots for eyes and work smile with stem stitch.

Step 7. Finish construction of sleeper according to pattern directions.

Step 8. Use hook-and-loop dot for closure instead of recommended button.

Step 9. Tie at bottom of sleeper is optional. ■

NIGHTIE
NIGHT
GIRAFFE
SLEEPER

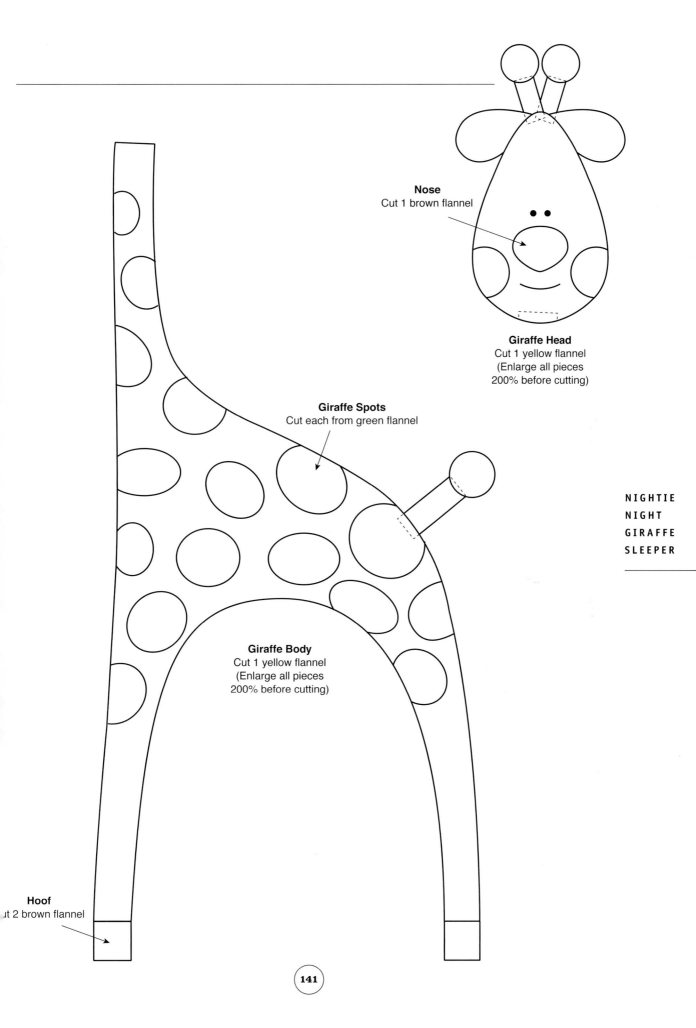

Nose
Cut 1 brown flannel

Giraffe Head
Cut 1 yellow flannel
(Enlarge all pieces
200% before cutting)

Giraffe Spots
Cut each from green flannel

Giraffe Body
Cut 1 yellow flannel
(Enlarge all pieces
200% before cutting)

Hoof
ut 2 brown flannel

NIGHTIE
NIGHT
GIRAFFE
SLEEPER

Flannel Diaper Bag & Accessories By Holly Daniels

Babies … soft … flannel—what a perfect combination!

Project Specifications
Skill Level: Beginner
Diaper Bag Size: Approximately 14$\frac{1}{2}$ x 12$\frac{1}{2}$ x 4$\frac{1}{2}$ inches

Materials
- $\frac{1}{2}$ yard blue print flannel
- 1 yard blue-and-yellow striped flannel
- 1 yard yellow solid flannel
- 14-inch yellow zipper
- Craft-size fusible batting
- Water-soluble marker
- Fusible web 4 x 8 inches
- 6-inch length of $\frac{1}{4}$-inch-wide elastic
- 1-inch dot of hook-and-loop tape
- All-purpose threads to match fabrics
- Basic sewing supplies and tools

Instructions

DIAPER BAG

Step 1. From blue-and-yellow striped flannel, cut two pieces 15 x 13 inches. From blue print flannel, cut four pieces 3$\frac{1}{2}$ x 15 inches.

Step 2. Mark striped flannel pieces 3$\frac{1}{4}$ inches from each long edge. Right sides facing, align blue print flannel strip with marked line and stitch with $\frac{1}{4}$-inch seam allowance as shown in **Fig. 1**. Flip the blue fabric down to cover the bottom portion of the striped fabric; press.

Repeat with each blue strip sewn along each long edge of both striped pieces as shown in **Fig. 2**.

Step 3. From yellow flannel, cut one pocket piece 7$\frac{3}{4}$ x 4 inches. From blue print flannel, cut one piece 4$\frac{3}{4}$ x 3$\frac{1}{4}$ inches. Fold under $\frac{1}{4}$ inch on all edges of both pieces; press. Stitch one long edge of each piece for upper hems.

Step 4. Center blue pocket on top of yellow pocket. Sew three unhemmed edges to yellow pocket as shown in **Fig. 3**. Center pocket on one striped side of bag. Sew three unhemmed edges to bag.

Step 5. From yellow solid flannel and fusible batting, cut two pieces each 15 x 13 inches.

Step 6. Place yellow solid flannel lining right side down on work surface. Place batting on yellow lining. Place pieced front and back right

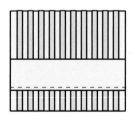

Fig. 1 Sew blue strip to striped rectangle as shown.

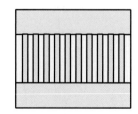

Fig. 1 Flip blue strips to cover edges of striped rectangle.

side up on top of batting. Following manufacturer's instructions, fuse fabrics to batting.

Step 7. For bag bottom, cut one piece each 15 x 5 inches from blue print flannel, yellow solid flannel and fusible batting. Layer as above and fuse.

Step 8. From blue print flannel, cut two pieces 15 x 3$^1/_2$ inches. Place right sides together and machine-baste $^1/_2$ inch from raw edge on one long side. Press the seam open.

Step 9. Center zipper on fabric strip with right side of zipper against seam. Baste zipper to seam allowance. Stitch $^1/_4$ inch each side of seam. Press lightly from right side. Remove basting stitches.

Step 10. From blue print flannel, cut two pieces 5 x 3 inches. Right sides facing, place across ends of zipper and stitch as shown in **Fig. 4** with $^1/_4$-inch seam allowance. Flip blue fabric back to cover ends of zipper panel. Trim entire piece to 5 x 15 inches; press.

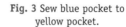
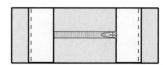

Fig. 3 Sew blue pocket to yellow pocket.

Fig. 4 Place blue strips against ends of zipper and stitch as shown.

Step 11. For the sides of the bag, cut two pieces each 5 x 13 inches from blue-and-yellow striped flannel, yellow solid flannel and fusible batting.

Step 12. From blue print flannel, cut four pieces 5 x 3$\frac{1}{2}$ inches. Sew the blue pieces to the top and bottom of the striped pieces as in Step 2. Layer with batting and lining and fuse as in Step 6.

Step 13. For strap, cut one piece each 5 x 37 inches from batting and striped and yellow flannel. Fuse layers as in Step 6.

Step 14. Pin the sides to the strap along the 5-inch ends, with seams going away from the inside of the bag. Sew with $\frac{1}{4}$-inch seam allowance. Sew bag bottom to remaining 5-inch ends of sides.

Step 15. From blue print flannel, cut four pieces for binding 2 x 5 inches. Sew to each seam to cover the raw edges.

Step 16. Sew the bag front, zipper panel and back together along the top of the bag with seams going away from bag. From blue print flannel, cut two pieces for binding 2 x 15 inches. Bind the raw edges.

Step 17. Pin the body of the bag to the strap/side/bottom piece with the seams going away from the bag. From blue-and-yellow striped flannel, cut two pieces for binding 2 x 75 inches, piecing as necessary. (Blue print flannel was used for part of bag bottom binding in model.) Bind raw edges of bag bottom, sides and strap.

BOTTLE BAG

Step 1. From blue-and-yellow striped flannel, yellow solid flannel and fusible batting, cut one piece each 8 x 11 inches. Fuse the layers together.

Step 2. Fold the fused piece in half, bringing short ends together, striped fabrics facing. Sew with $\frac{1}{4}$-inch seam allowance to form tube.

Step 3. From blue-and-yellow striped flannel, cut a circle 5 inches in diameter. Pin, right sides facing, to opening at one end of tube. Sew with $\frac{1}{4}$-inch seam allowance. Clip curves to allow to lie flat.

Step 4. From yellow solid flannel, cut a strip 2$\frac{1}{2}$ x 11 inches for a binding/elastic casing. Fold one short edge over $\frac{1}{4}$ inch. Fold strip in half lengthwise.

Step 5. Align raw edges of binding strip with top raw edge of tube, right sides facing. Pin to tube, starting with the short end that is folded under. End by layering the loose end of the binding over the fold. Trim excess length and fold raw end under $\frac{1}{4}$ inch. Stitch with $\frac{1}{4}$-inch seam allowance.

Step 6. Fold binding to inside of bag and stitch in place by hand, leaving folded ends open.

Step 7. Thread the 6-inch length of $\frac{1}{4}$-inch-wide elastic through opening and stitch ends together to secure.

BIB

Step 1. Cut fabric for bib as instructed on pattern.

Step 2. Trace hearts on paper side of fusible web. Cut out, leaving roughly $\frac{1}{4}$-inch margin around traced lines. Following manufacturer's instructions, fuse to selected fabrics. Cut out on traced lines.

Step 3. Referring to photo for placement, arrange hearts on striped bib; fuse. Stitch around hearts with matching threads using machine satin stitch or blanket stitch.

Step 4. Make 1¼ yards of 1½-inch-wide bias strips from yellow solid flannel. Fold in half lengthwise for binding.

Step 5. Layer bib pieces, wrong sides facing; pin or baste. Apply binding to raw edges, beginning and ending at back of bib.

Step 6. Sew hook-and-loop dots to overlapping back flaps of bib. ■

Bib
Cut 1 stripe & 1 yellow

Place line on fold

Small Heart
Cut 1 yellow

Large Heart
Cut 1 blue

My First Dollies

By Diana Stunell-Dunsmore

Make these two plump fleecy companions to delight your little one!

Project Specifications
Skill Level: Beginner
Doll Sizes: Approximately $8^1/_2$ x $10^1/_2$ inches

Materials
Note: Materials are for each doll
- Scraps of medium pink fleece for appliqué
- $^1/_4$ yard light pink lambskin fleece
- $^1/_4$ yard light blue lambskin fleece for piggy's hooded shirt
- $^3/_8$ yard light blue print flannelette for baby's hooded bunting
- Scraps of fusible interfacing
- Scraps of fusible web
- Bag of polyester fiberfill
- Medium blue, black and dark pink 6-strand embroidery floss
- All-purpose threads to match fabrics
- $3^1/_2$-inch piece of $^1/_4$-inch-wide elastic
- Medium-length strong needle
- Small pliers, optional
- Basic sewing supplies and tools

Instructions

PIGGY

Step 1. Cut out fabric pieces according to pattern instructions. Transfer markings to body pieces only, not clothing.

Step 2. Sew two arms, right sides together, leaving ends open as shown on pattern. Sew legs. Trim seams, clip curves and corners. Turn right side out.

Step 3. Push a small amount of fiberfill into ends of each leg. Machine-stitch on short lines of legs to form hooves. Finish stuffing legs and arms. Baste open ends to close edges. Clip curves of basted edges if necessary.

Step 4. Position arms and legs to body front as indicated on pattern; pin.

Step 5. Pin one end of $3^1/_2$-inch piece of $^1/_4$-inch-wide elastic to tail at marked position and as shown in **Fig. 1**. Fold tail in half lengthwise. Sew across end where tail is pinned and down other long edge. Leave open at other short end. Sew over elastic several times to secure firmly. Turn right side out. Turn raw edge up inside tail $^1/_4$ inch. Pull on elastic until tail has desired curl. Trim elastic $^3/_8$ inch beyond the end of the turned-up edge. Fold the extra $^3/_8$-inch end of elastic up into the tail and machine-stitch across the end of the tail through all layers. Machine-stitch in place on body back.

Step 6. Pin body front to body back, right sides facing. Sew around body with arms and legs enclosed. Leave neck edge open. Trim seam, clip curves at arms and legs. Turn right side out and stuff firmly. As you reach the top, turn under neck edge ¹/₄ inch; stuff full.

Step 7. Cut two interfacing pieces for piggy's ears. Fuse to wrong side of each ear front. Sew ears, right sides facing, leaving bottom edge open. Trim seams and corners; clip curves. Turn right side out.

Step 8. Using doubled thread, hand-gather around face close to edge. Pull thread up till face is about the size of the solid face line on the pattern. Place a ball of fiberfill in the center and adjust thread and fiberfill, adding more if necessary until it has the right shape; knot off.

Step 9. Form the snout in the same manner as the face. Knot off, but do not cut thread. With 3 strands of black embroidery floss, stitch nostrils. Pull tight and knot off.

Step 10. Attach snout to face using long running stitches worked ladder-style through snout and face as shown in **Fig. 2**. Sew around the snout at least three times to secure it very well for safe baby use. Knot off securely.

Step 11. Use 6 strands of medium blue embroidery floss and make two triple-wrapped French knots for piggy's eyes. Knot off very securely. Small pliers may be useful to pull the thick

floss through the fleece and stuffing. Be sure to secure the stitches through both front and back layers of fabric.

Step 12. Position ears to back of face as indicated on pattern and sew securely in place along open edges of ears, using doubled thread.

Step 13. Trace heart on fusible web. Cut out, leaving roughly ¹/₄-inch margin around traced line. Following manufacturer's instructions, fuse to medium pink fleece. Cut out on traced lines and fuse to blue fleece shirt front.

Step 14. With matching thread, zigzag around edges of heart.

Step 15. Clip to seam at shirt underarm as shown on pattern. Place shirt front and back together, right sides facing, and sew shoulder seams, leaving neck open between marks. Press seams open. Press under ¹/₄ inch along armhole edges; stitch.

Step 16. Turn up ¹/₂-inch hem on lower edge of shirt, press and sew. Sew side seams, right sides facing. Press seams open. Turn shirt right side out. Pull shirt over pig's neck and pull arms through armholes.

Step 17. Align raw neck edge of body with shirt. Fold layers under together ³/₈ inch and pin all around. With doubled thread, take running stitches all around the upper neck edge at least twice, making certain to sew through clothing and body layers. Remember it must be very

Fig. 1 Position elastic tail as shown.

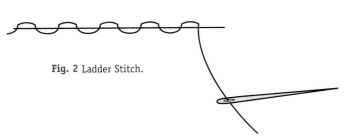

Fig. 2 Ladder Stitch.

secure for baby safety. Pull up gathers leaving a 1-inch hole; knot off.

Step 18. Sew one long hood gusset edge to top edge of one hood piece, right sides facing and matching points. Sew from straight edge only to dot at point. Sew the other long edge of gusset to the remaining hood piece the same way. Clip curves if necessary; trim point. Sew back of hood from round mark at point to square mark near lower edge. Clip curves. Press seams open as much as possible.

Step 19. Press under ⅝-inch seam allowance along front straight edge of hood. Set face into hood. Pin straight edge of hood to outside edge of face. Bring lower edges of hood farther back under face. These raw edges will be concealed during construction. Using a single strand of thread, carefully sew a running stitch ladder-style through face and front edge of hood. This stitching is not meant to show. Run this stitching around the face twice for extra security. Sew only through the back layer of the ears when you come to them.

Step 20. Stuff hood firmly. Turn under raw edge ¼ inch and pin. Hand-gather using doubled thread; pull up and knot thread but do not cut.

Step 21. Pin head to body. Sew with long ladder-style running stitches around the head several times. It should feel very stable and secure and all raw edges and openings should be completely covered. Knot off neatly in back.

BABY BUNTING

Step 1. Repeat Steps 1–4 for Piggy, except do not make stitches in legs to form hooves.

Step 2. Repeat Step 6 for body.

Step 3. Using a single strand of matching thread, hand-gather around the edge of each cheek. Pull thread up till cheek is the size of the cheek line on the pattern piece. Spread the gathers until the cheeks are smooth and round. Knot off, but do not cut thread. Neatly hand-appliqué onto face.

Step 4. With 3 strands of dark pink embroidery floss, securely knotted on the back of the face, embroider baby's mouth with a split stitch. With medium blue embroidery floss, embroider the eyes.

Step 5. Appliqué heart to bunting as in Steps 13–14, Piggy.

Step 6. Clip to seam at underarm marks on bunting as shown on pattern. Zigzag-stitch around armhole edges of bunting to finish. Sew front to back, right sides facing, from armholes to triangles along lower edge.

Step 7. Pull bunting on over baby. Clip curves, turn right side out and press. Press up seam allowances of open end as well. Push baby's body up into bunting through opening. Pull arms through armholes. Pin bunting closed at bottom. Neatly ladder-stitch bunting closed.

Step 8. Follow Steps 17–21 to finish baby same as piggy. ∎

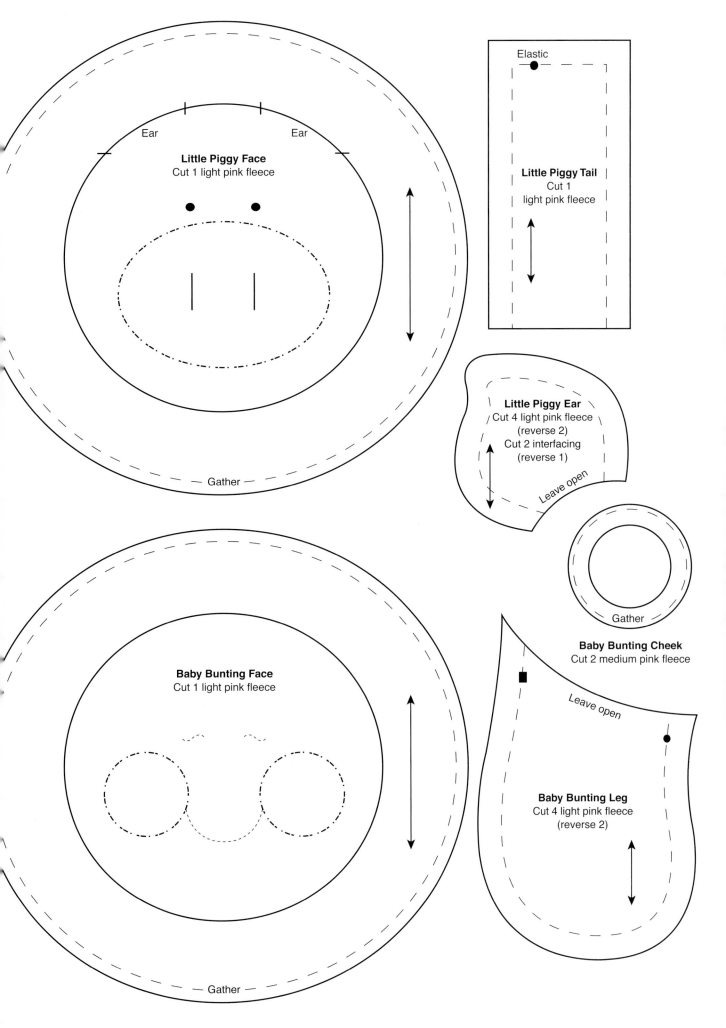

Little Piggy Face
Cut 1 light pink fleece

Ear Ear

Gather

Little Piggy Tail
Cut 1
light pink fleece

Elastic

Little Piggy Ear
Cut 4 light pink fleece
(reverse 2)
Cut 2 interfacing
(reverse 1)

Leave open

Baby Bunting Cheek
Cut 2 medium pink fleece

Gather

Baby Bunting Face
Cut 1 light pink fleece

Gather

Baby Bunting Leg
Cut 4 light pink fleece
(reverse 2)

Leave open

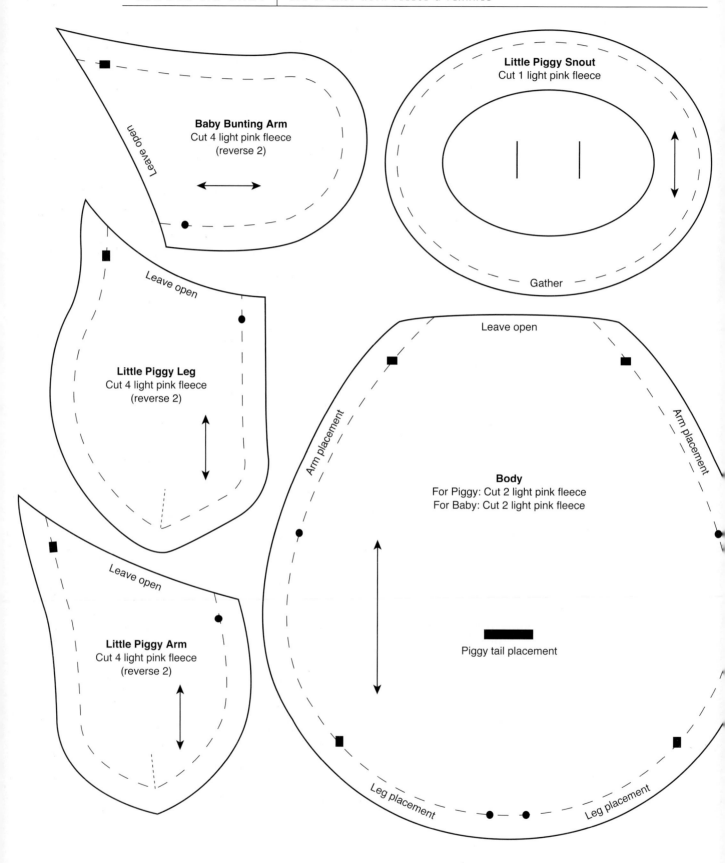

Baby Bunting Arm
Cut 4 light pink fleece
(reverse 2)

Leave open

Little Piggy Snout
Cut 1 light pink fleece

Gather

Leave open

Little Piggy Leg
Cut 4 light pink fleece
(reverse 2)

Leave open

Arm placement

Arm placement

Body
For Piggy: Cut 2 light pink fleece
For Baby: Cut 2 light pink fleece

Piggy tail placement

Little Piggy Arm
Cut 4 light pink fleece
(reverse 2)

Leave open

Leg placement

Leg placement

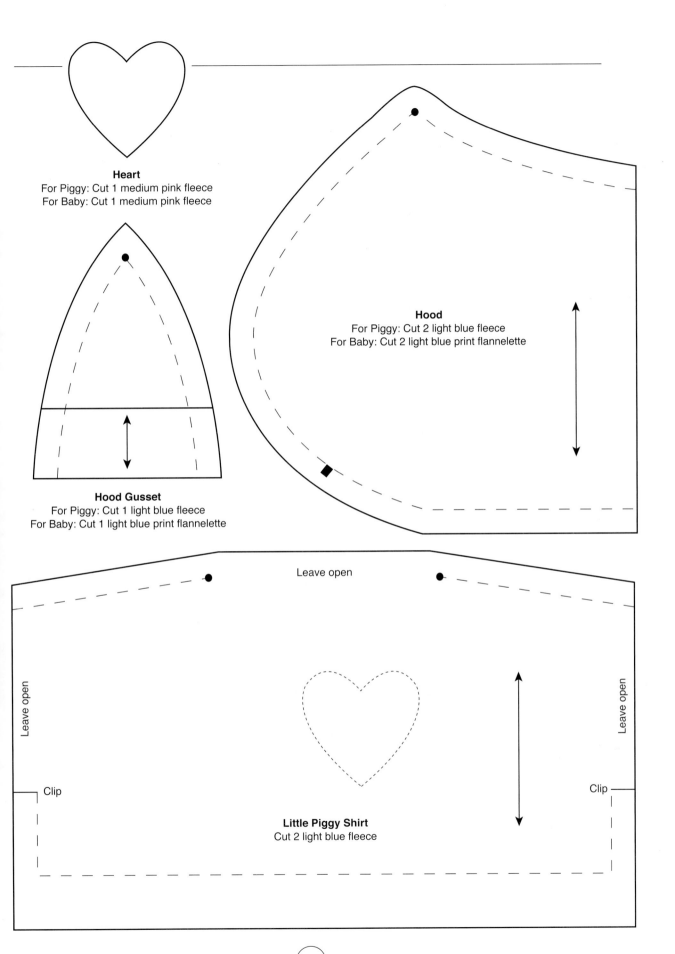

Heart
For Piggy: Cut 1 medium pink fleece
For Baby: Cut 1 medium pink fleece

Hood
For Piggy: Cut 2 light blue fleece
For Baby: Cut 2 light blue print flannelette

Hood Gusset
For Piggy: Cut 1 light blue fleece
For Baby: Cut 1 light blue print flannelette

Leave open

Leave open

Leave open

Clip

Clip

Little Piggy Shirt
Cut 2 light blue fleece

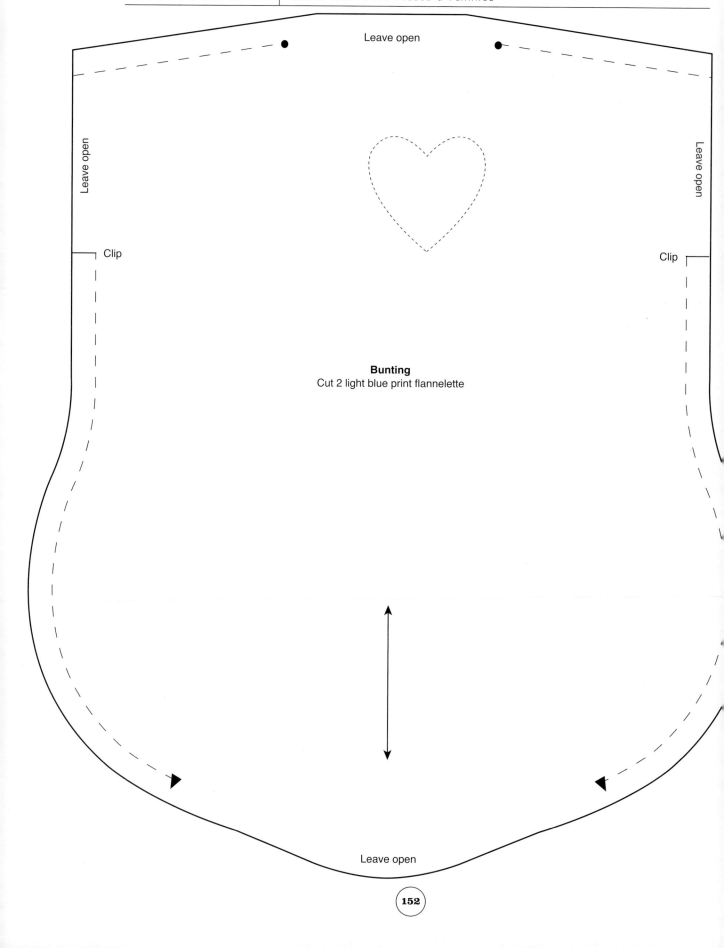

Leave open

Leave open

Leave open

Clip

Clip

Bunting
Cut 2 light blue print flannelette

Leave open

Barnyard Play Pad & Finger Puppets

By Connie Matricardi

Your toddler will love being in the center of this cute personal barnyard.

Project Specifications
Skill Level: Beginner
Play Pad Size: 30 x 36 inches

Materials

- Light blue fleece 30 x 36 inches for background
- Hunter green fleece circle 20 inches in diameter
- Scraps of brown and hunter green fleece for trees
- Coordinating flannel for backing 30 x 36 inches
- 9 x 12-inch rectangle each of red, white, black, pink, tan, yellow and gray felt
- 2 packages black medium rickrack
- 1 package 1/4-inch-wide black twill tape
- 2 packages light blue double-fold quilt binding
- All-purpose threads to match fabrics
- 1 (3/4-inch) black hook-and-loop dot
- 1 (3/4-inch) white hook-and-loop dot
- Air-soluble marker
- 2 (5mm) pink pompoms
- 3 (5mm) black pompoms
- Black dimensional paint pen
- Fabric glue
- Newsprint or pattern paper 20 x 20 inches
- Hot-glue gun and glue sticks
- Basic sewing supplies and tools

Instructions

PLAY PAD

Step 1. Round the corners of the light blue background fleece rectangle.

Step 2. Place and pin hunter green fleece circle to light blue background rectangle. Circle should be approximately 4³/₄ inches from side and bottom edges of background. Baste in place ⁵/₈ inch from raw edges.

Step 3. Press black twill tape and cut 11 six-inch lengths for barnyard fence posts. Fold each length in half, bringing short ends together. Referring to photo for placement, position fence posts around barnyard circle. Pin in place, tucking raw edges of fence posts under circle ½ inch. With light blue thread in the bobbin and black in the needle, stitch in place. **_Note:_** _Keep blue thread in bobbin throughout and change thread in needle as needed._

Step 4. Position black rickrack 1 inch from barnyard edges as shown in photo. Pin in place. Position another row of rickrack 1 inch from the first row. Stitch to background.

Step 5. Trace and cut appliqué shapes as instructed on patterns. From white felt, cut a 3½ x 8½-inch rectangle for silo. Cut a 1½ x 3-inch rectangle from black felt for silo door. For barn window, cut a 1½ x 1½-inch black felt square. For barn door, cut a 4½ x 5-inch rectangle from black felt and a 2¼ x 5-inch rectangle from gray felt.

BARNYARD PLAY PAD & FINGER PUPPETS

Step 6. Stitch three apples to each treetop. Pin tree trunks and treetops to background as shown in photo. Tuck ends of tree trunks under edge of barnyard circle and under treetops.

Step 7. Stitch door and heart to doghouse. Stitch one portion of black hook-and-loop dot to door. Cut and stitch a 5¾-inch length of twill tape to top of doghouse for roof. Turn ends under ½ inch. Wrap around felt of doghouse and stitch to secure. Pin doghouse to background, tucking lower edge under barnyard circle ½ inch.

Step 8. Stitch silo door to silo. Stitch one portion of white hook-and-loop dot to door. Stitch a 4¾-inch length of black twill tape across the bottom edge of the silo roof. Position and pin silo and roof to background. Position so silo base is on top of barnyard circle ½ inch.

Step 9. For the barn door, cut two 8-inch lengths and one 3-inch length of black twill tape. Position and pin the 8-inch lengths to the gray felt rectangle in a V and an inverted V, wrapping ends to back of door. Refer to the photo for placement. Stitch in place. Place the 3-inch strip of twill tape vertically in the center of the door and stitch. This completes the lower barn door.

Step 10. Stitch completed lower barn door to black barn door, leaving upper edge of gray door open to form pocket for puppets. Stitch completed door to barn. Stitch window to barn.

Step 11. Stitch a 15-inch length of black twill tape to the barn top edge as a roof. Stitch a 5-inch length of black twill tape to top of cupola for roof.

Step 12. Position and pin barn and cupola to background. Position so barn base is on top of barnyard circle ½ inch. Tuck cupola under barn roof. Stitch barn and cupola to background.

Step 13. Pin play pad and backing together, wrong sides facing. Stitch barnyard to backing and fleece layers. Stitch near edge of barnyard circle.

Step 14. Bind play pad with light blue double-fold quilt binding.

PUPPETS

Step 1. Trace and cut all puppet pieces as instructed on patterns.

Step 2. Stitch remaining portion of white hook-and-loop dot to back of chicken body. Stitch remaining black hook-and-loop dot to back of dog body. Insert dog tail between dog body front and back.

Step 3. With white thread and 1/8-inch seam allowance, wrong sides facing, stitch each puppet body together. Leave bottom edges open.

Step 4. Position each puppet head front so that it overlaps the body about 1/2 inch. Insert dog's tongue under head. Glue head fronts to bodies. Glue any other head parts, such as horns, beak, comb, to back of head. Add face details with black dimensional paint pen.

Step 5. For pig, glue second head to back of head front. Glue pig nose to head. Glue pink pompoms to nose. Hot glue works best with pompoms.

Step 6. For cow, glue second head to back of head front. Glue tan ears to front of cow head. Glue tan spots to cow front. Glue two black pompoms to cow head as nostrils.

Step 7. For goat, glue second head to back

of head front. Glue nose in place.

Step 8. For chicken, glue second head to back of head front. Glue wing to puppet front.

Step 9. For dog, glue second head to back of head front. Glue a black pompom to face for nose. Glue black spots to dog front.

Step 10. Attach dog to doghouse and chicken to silo with hook-and-loop dots. Place pig, cow and goat in barn door pocket. ■

BARNYARD
PLAY PAD &
FINGER
PUPPETS

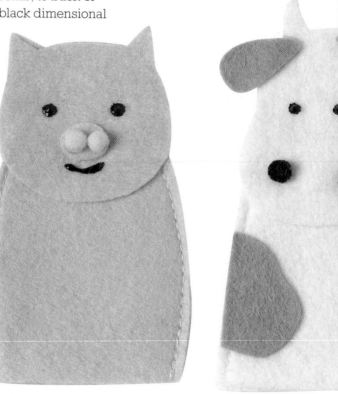

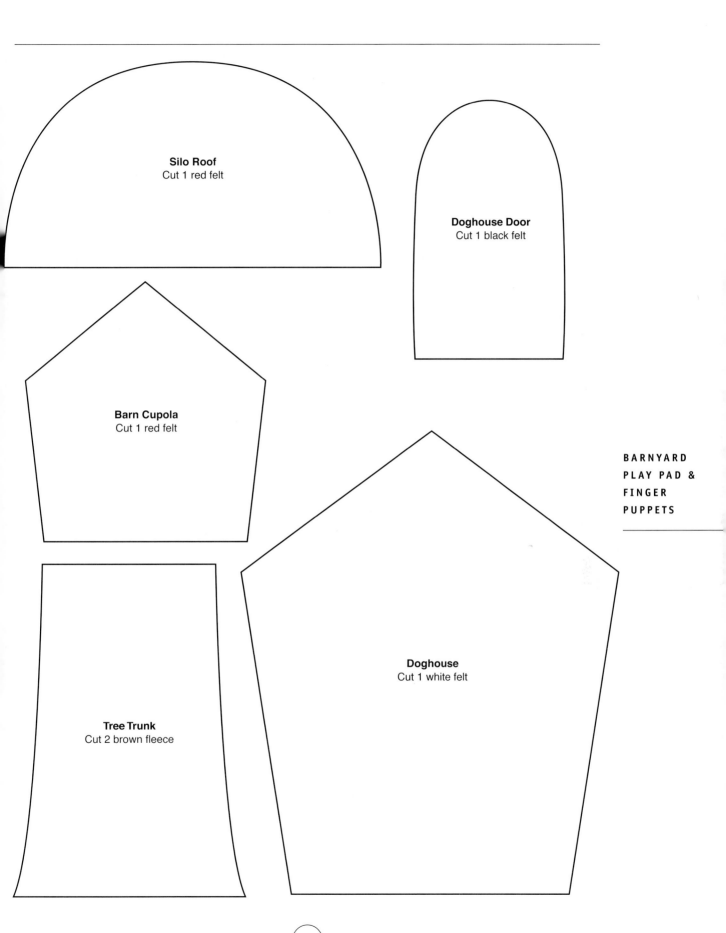

Silo Roof
Cut 1 red felt

Doghouse Door
Cut 1 black felt

Barn Cupola
Cut 1 red felt

Doghouse
Cut 1 white felt

Tree Trunk
Cut 2 brown fleece

BARNYARD
PLAY PAD &
FINGER
PUPPETS

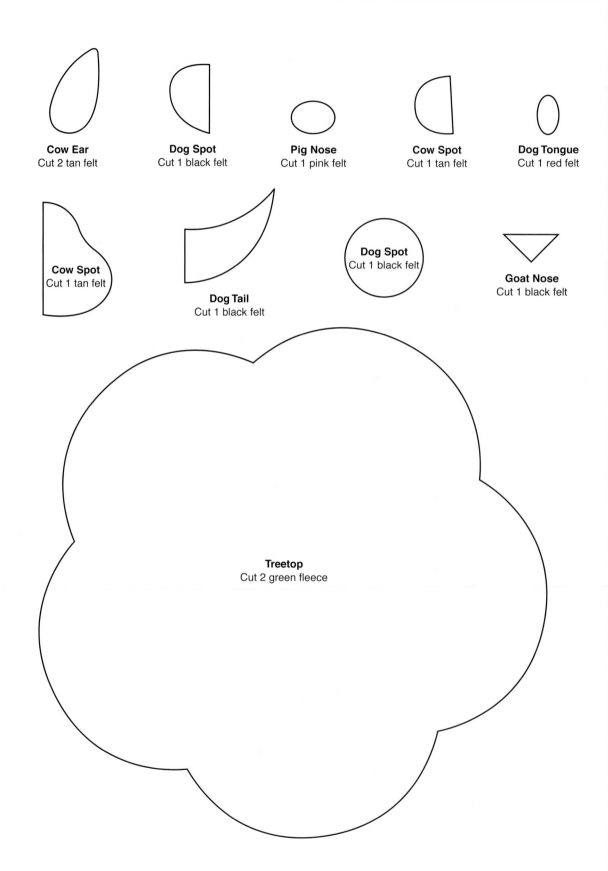

Cow Ear
Cut 2 tan felt

Dog Spot
Cut 1 black felt

Pig Nose
Cut 1 pink felt

Cow Spot
Cut 1 tan felt

Dog Tongue
Cut 1 red felt

Cow Spot
Cut 1 tan felt

Dog Tail
Cut 1 black felt

Dog Spot
Cut 1 black felt

Goat Nose
Cut 1 black felt

BARNYARD PLAY PAD & FINGER PUPPETS

Treetop
Cut 2 green fleece

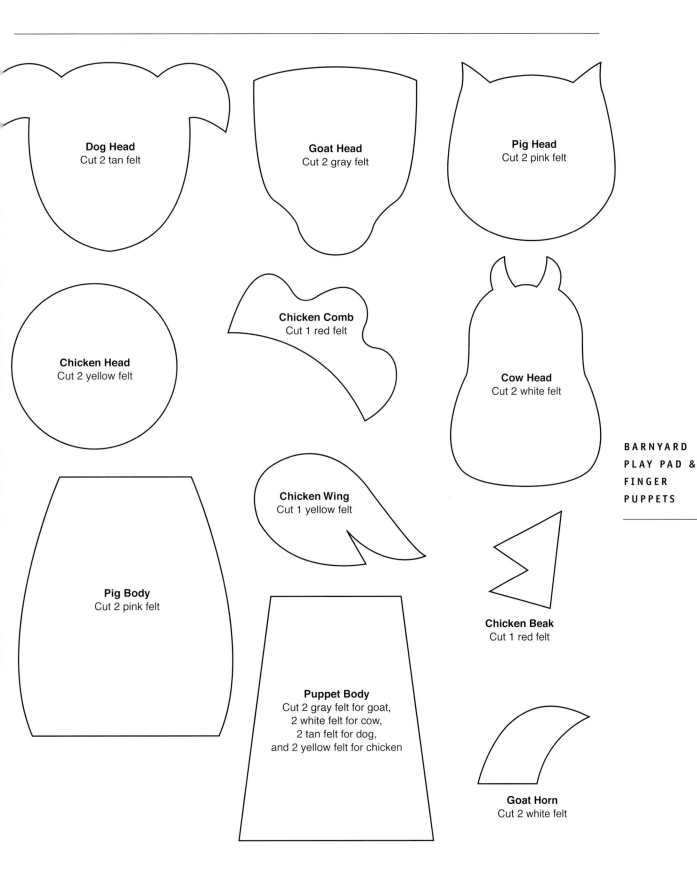

Dog Head
Cut 2 tan felt

Goat Head
Cut 2 gray felt

Pig Head
Cut 2 pink felt

Chicken Head
Cut 2 yellow felt

Chicken Comb
Cut 1 red felt

Cow Head
Cut 2 white felt

Pig Body
Cut 2 pink felt

Chicken Wing
Cut 1 yellow felt

Chicken Beak
Cut 1 red felt

Puppet Body
Cut 2 gray felt for goat,
2 white felt for cow,
2 tan felt for dog,
and 2 yellow felt for chicken

Goat Horn
Cut 2 white felt

BARNYARD
PLAY PAD &
FINGER
PUPPETS

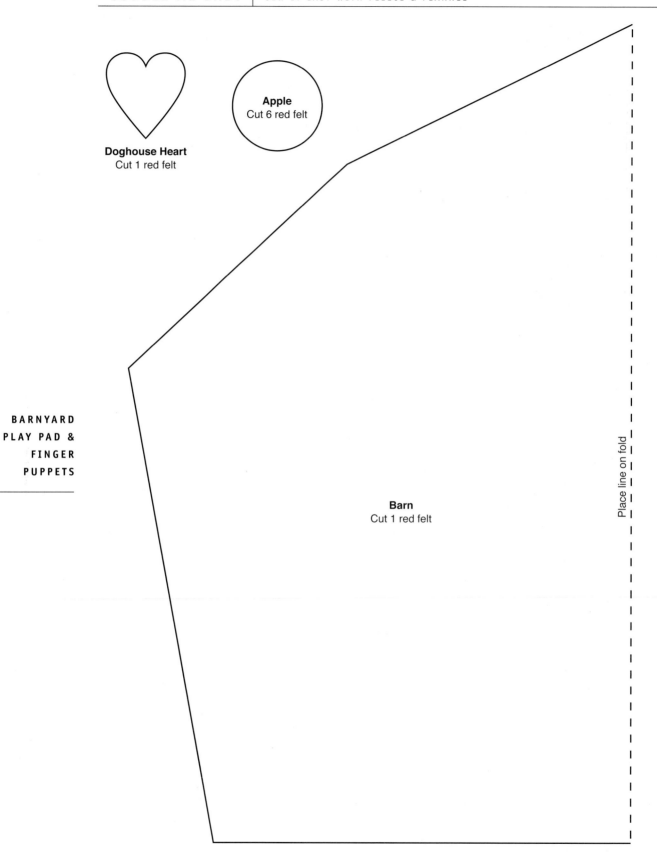

Doghouse Heart
Cut 1 red felt

Apple
Cut 6 red felt

**BARNYARD
PLAY PAD &
FINGER
PUPPETS**

Barn
Cut 1 red felt

Place line on fold

Baby's Cuddle Blanket

By Diana Stunell-Dunsmore

Fleecy white sheep frolic across this soft blanket, entertaining and warming baby.

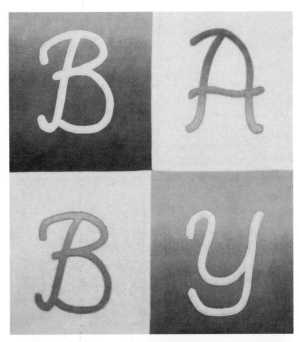

Project Specifications
Skill Level: Beginner
Blanket Size: 34 x 40 inches

Materials
- $1/8$ yard pink lambskin fleece
- $3/8$ yard white lambskin fleece
- 2 yards blue variegated lambskin fleece
- 1 yard fusible web
- All-purpose threads to match fabrics
- Medium blue and medium pink 6-strand embroidery floss
- Basic sewing supplies and tools

Instructions
Step 1. From blue variegated lambskin fleece, cut two blanket panels $35^{1}/_{4}$ x $41^{1}/_{4}$ inches. This includes $5/_{8}$-inch seam allowance. Set aside.

Step 2. Trace appliqué shapes on paper side of fusible web as instructed on patterns. Cut out, leaving roughly $1/_{4}$-inch margin around traced shapes.

Step 3. Following manufacturer's instructions, fuse pieces to selected fabrics. Because of the

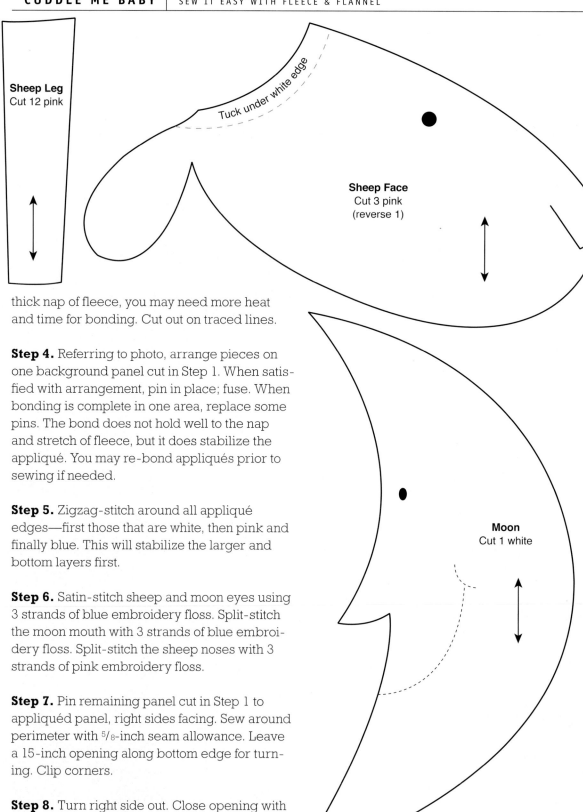

Sheep Leg
Cut 12 pink

Sheep Face
Cut 3 pink
(reverse 1)

Tuck under white edge

Moon
Cut 1 white

thick nap of fleece, you may need more heat and time for bonding. Cut out on traced lines.

Step 4. Referring to photo, arrange pieces on one background panel cut in Step 1. When satisfied with arrangement, pin in place; fuse. When bonding is complete in one area, replace some pins. The bond does not hold well to the nap and stretch of fleece, but it does stabilize the appliqué. You may re-bond appliqués prior to sewing if needed.

BABY'S CUDDLE BLANKET

Step 5. Zigzag-stitch around all appliqué edges—first those that are white, then pink and finally blue. This will stabilize the larger and bottom layers first.

Step 6. Satin-stitch sheep and moon eyes using 3 strands of blue embroidery floss. Split-stitch the moon mouth with 3 strands of blue embroidery floss. Split-stitch the sheep noses with 3 strands of pink embroidery floss.

Step 7. Pin remaining panel cut in Step 1 to appliquéd panel, right sides facing. Sew around perimeter with ⅝-inch seam allowance. Leave a 15-inch opening along bottom edge for turning. Clip corners.

Step 8. Turn right side out. Close opening with hand stitches. ◼

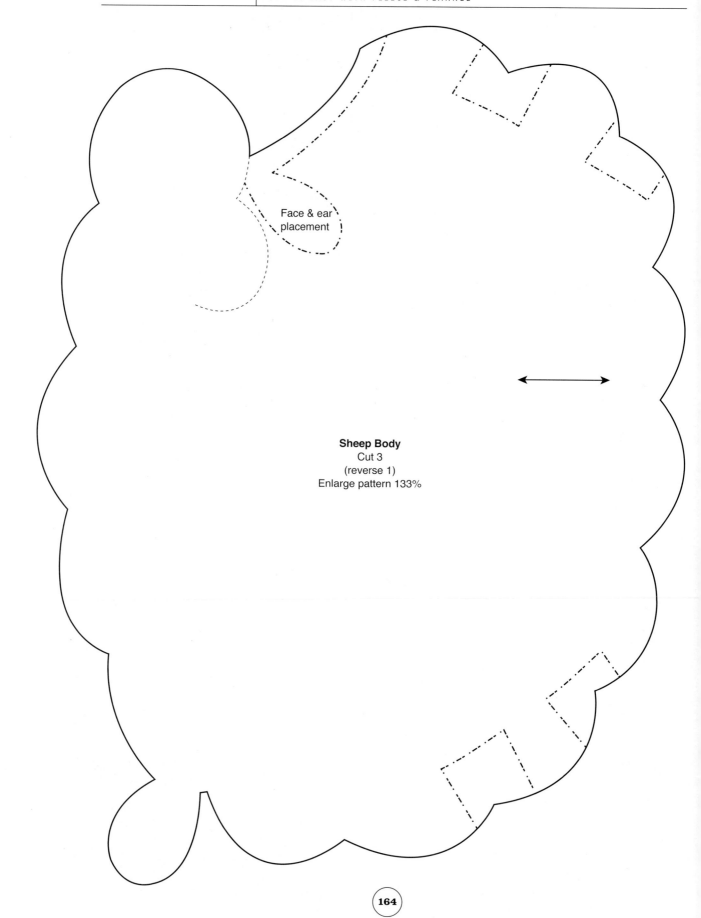

Face & ear
placement

Sheep Body
Cut 3
(reverse 1)
Enlarge pattern 133%

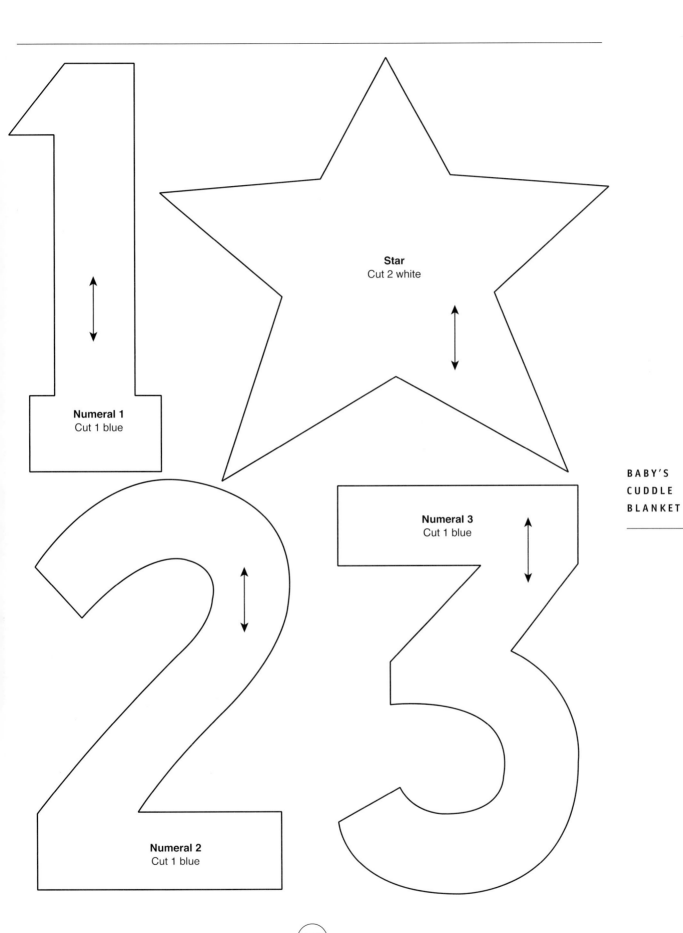

Numeral 1
Cut 1 blue

Star
Cut 2 white

Numeral 3
Cut 1 blue

Numeral 2
Cut 1 blue

Sea Buddies By Bev Shenefield

Not for the tub—these soft, fuzzy creatures are landlubbers.

Project Specifications

Skill Level: Beginner
Fish Size: Approximately 10 x 5 inches
Octopus Size: Approximately 6 x 9 inches

Materials

- Scrap of aqua flannel
- Scrap of orange knit fleece
- 18-inch square of lavender fleece
- 2 pieces yellow fleece 8 x 12 inches
- $1/8$ yard each of at least 15 different plain and printed flannels
- 1-inch-thick soft foam 10 x 12 inches
- Natural buttonhole thread
- All-purpose threads to match fabrics
- Aqua, black, orange and ecru 6-strand embroidery floss
- 1 package white elastic cord
- 1 very soft ball 5 inches in diameter
- Embroidery needle
- Large-eyed needle
- Pinking shears
- Basic sewing supplies and tools

Instructions

FISHY WISHY

Step 1. Use fish pattern to cut one fish from 1-inch-thick foam. Cut two layers of yellow fleece $1^1/2$ inches larger on all sides than foam.

Step 2. Place one fleece fish face down on work surface. Top fleece with foam fish. Place remaining fleece fish right side up on top of foam fish. Sew around perimeter by machine. Trim close to seam with pinking shears.

Step 3. Cut mouth and eyes as instructed on pattern.

Step 4. Position mouth pieces on each side of fish. With 6 strands of orange embroidery floss, work buttonhole stitch around all edges on each side of yellow fleece and to each other on extended portion.

Step 5. Position aqua portion of eyes and work buttonhole stitch around shape with 6 strands of aqua embroidery floss.

Step 6. Place orange eyelids over eye and pin. With 6 strands of black embroidery floss, start just above lower edge of eyelid and work pupil of eye with satin stitch. With 6 strands of ecru embroidery floss, add a few stitches near pupil to highlight. With 6 strands of orange embroidery floss, stitch eyelid in place with buttonhole stitch. With stem stitch, add a black line along the lower edge of eyelid and add lashes as shown on pattern.

YO-YO OCTOPUS

Step 1. From lavender fleece, cut one circle each $13^3/4$ inches in diameter and $2^3/4$ inches in diameter.

Step 2. From the variety of flannels, cut 120 circles 2³/₄ inches in diameter. From aqua flannel, cut two octopus eyes.

Step 3. Fold the large lavender circle in half. Make a dart that is 2 inches wide at the outside of the circle and tapers to a point 5³/₄ inches in as shown in **Fig. 1**. Repeat on the other side.

Step 4. Fold the circle the other direction and make one dart as before, but instead of ending at the 5³/₄-inch point, continue across the center and back to 2 inches on the opposite side as shown in **Fig. 2**.

Step 5. Place the circle over the soft ball, right side out. Adjust as needed. Remove ball and sew gathering stitch around edge with buttonhole thread. Insert ball and pull up gathers tightly. Use overhand knot to make sure thread will stay in place. Cover the opening with the smaller lavender fleece circle sewn in place around circumference.

Step 6. Turn edges of flannel circles under slightly and gather edges with buttonhole thread. Fasten thread with overhand knot. Smooth out into flat yo-yo circle.

Step 7. Tie a knot in the end of a piece of elastic cord. String 15 yo-yos with open side up, mixing a variety of colors and prints. Attach cord to edge of small lavender fleece circle, pull up to 3¹/₄ inches in length and tie knot.

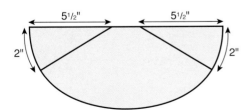

Fig. 1 Make dart as shown.

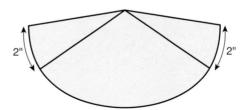

Fig. 2 Stitch as shown.

Step 8. Repeat and attach second leg directly across from first leg. Repeat for six more legs, attaching three legs each side of the first two legs for a total of eight evenly spaced legs.

Step 9. Referring to photo, position eyes on head and buttonhole-stitch in place with 6 strands of aqua embroidery floss. Fill in pupil of eye with 6 strands of black embroidery floss worked in satin stitch. Add several small stitches of ecru embroidery floss to highlight pupil.

Step 10. Referring to photo, draw smile on face. Use 6 strands of black embroidery floss and stem stitch to embroider the mouth.

Step 11. You may want to add a hoop of elastic cord at the top of the octopus head for hanging. ■

Octopus Eye
Cut 2 aqua flannel

SEA
BUDDIES

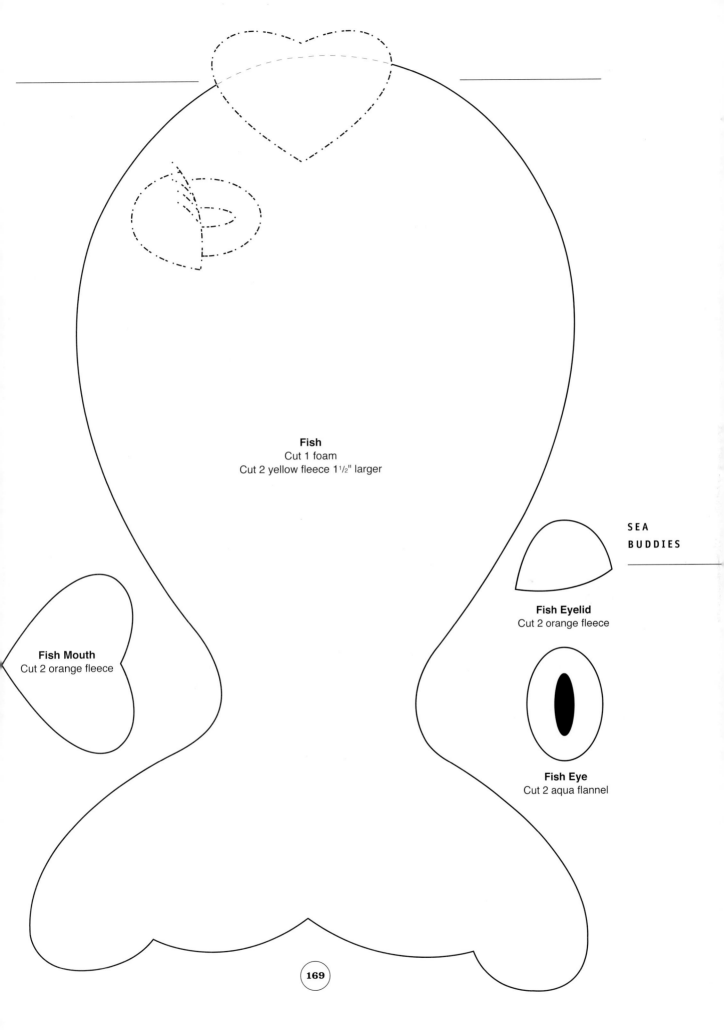

Fish
Cut 1 foam
Cut 2 yellow fleece 1½" larger

Fish Mouth
Cut 2 orange fleece

Fish Eyelid
Cut 2 orange fleece

Fish Eye
Cut 2 aqua flannel

SEA
BUDDIES

169

Rainbow Fish Baby Quilt & Mobile
By Judith Sandstrom

The brilliant colors of these aquarium fish are spectacular.

Project Specifications
Skill Level: Beginner
Quilt Size: 42 x 56 inches

Materials
- Scrap of black flannel for eyes
- $1/2$ yard each green, peach, pink, blue, yellow and lavender marble-finish cotton flannel
- $1^1/2$ yards marble-finish navy cotton flannel
- Flannel backing 46 x 60 inches
- Thin batting 46 x 60 inches
- 3 squares thin batting 6 x 6 inches
- $2^1/4$ yards fusible web
- $1/4$ yard tear-away stabilizer
- Pastel satin-covered hanger with swivel top
- Nylon monofilament or clear fishing line
- Rotary-cutting tools
- All-purpose threads to match fabrics
- Basic sewing supplies and tools

Instructions

QUILT

Step 1. Prewash and press all fabrics.

Step 2. From navy flannel, cut 12 squares 12 x 12 inches.

Step 3. From each of the six pastel flannels, cut three 2-inch-wide strips across the width of the fabric.

Step 4. Trace fish, stripes and eyes on paper side of fusible web as instructed on patterns. Cut out, leaving roughly $1/4$-inch margin around shapes. Following manufacturer's instructions, fuse to selected fabrics. Cut out on traced lines.

Step 5. Center a fish form on each 12-inch navy square and fuse. Place stripes on fish. Stripes are numbered 1–4 to indicate order from front to back of fish. Peach stripes go on green fish, blue stripes go on pink fish and lavender stripes go on yellow fish. Refer to photo and pattern for placement; align and fuse. Add eyes and fuse.

Step 6. Border strips cut in Step 2 are added to blocks in Log Cabin manner. Stitch a strip to the right side of block, trim the strip end even with the end of the block; press seam toward strip. Add another strip to the bottom of block in the same manner. Next, add a strip to the right side and then the top. Each block of a particular color fish has identical border strips added in the same order. Green and peach fish should be bordered yellow, blue, lavender and pink. Yellow and lavender fish should be bordered pink, green, blue and peach. Pink and blue fish should be bordered in peach, yellow, green and lavender.

Step 7. Using the photo as a guide, stitch the fish blocks together in four rows of three blocks each. Press all seams open.

Step 8. Smooth batting on large work surface. Center quilt top right side up over batting. Loosely hand-baste the edges together and trim away the excess batting. Remove quilt top from work surface.

Step 9. Place backing right side up on work surface. Center quilt top, right side down, on backing. Pin edges together. Stitch around the perimeter leaving a 12-inch opening in the center of one side for turning. Turn quilt right side out and press. Close opening with hand stitches.

Step 10. Machine-stitch in the ditch in vertical and horizontal rows between the blocks and in the ditch between the navy background and outer border around the perimeter. Also stitch $1/4$ inch from the outer edge around the perimeter.

Step 11. Using a medium-width zigazg stitch and thread to match, machine-appliqué the fish, stripes and eyes. Backstitch the ends to secure threads.

MOBILE

Step 1. Fold green, pink and yellow fabrics in half, right sides facing. Trace around mobile fish pattern on each folded fabric. Pin fabric layers together and cut fish out

$1/4$ inch outside traced lines. Clip curves and corners.

Step 2. Trace fish stripes and eyes on fusible web as instructed on patterns. Cut out, leaving roughly $1/4$-inch margin around traced lines. Fuse to selected fabrics and cut out on traced lines.

Step 3. Unpin fish pieces and place each on work surface right side up. Using fish pattern as a guide, place blue stripes on pink fish, lavender stripes on yellow fish and peach stripes on green fish; fuse. Place and fuse eyes.

Step 4. From tear-away stabilizer, cut six pieces 4 x 5 inches. Place a piece of stabilizer under the stripe/eye area of each fish piece. With matching thread, zigzag-stitch all the way around each strip and eye appliqué. Tear away the stabilizer.

Step 5. With right sides facing and raw edges aligned, place two fish of the same color on a 6-inch batting square; pin. Stitch on traced line through all thicknesses, leaving a 2-inch opening on the underside of the fish for turning. Trim batting even with flannel. Turn right side out and close opening with hand stitches.

Step 6. Cut nylon monofilament or fishing line in three 15-inch lengths. Securely tie one end to the top fin of each fish and attach the other end to the padded hanger. Thoroughly knot and draw the ends of the nylon inside the hanger and fish. The model has the center fish hanging 5 inches down from the hanger, and the other fish 7 and 9 inches from the hanger.

Step 7. Use double length of monofilament or fishing line to hang mobile at proper length from securely fastened ceiling hook. ■

RAINBOW FISH BABY QUILT & MOBILE

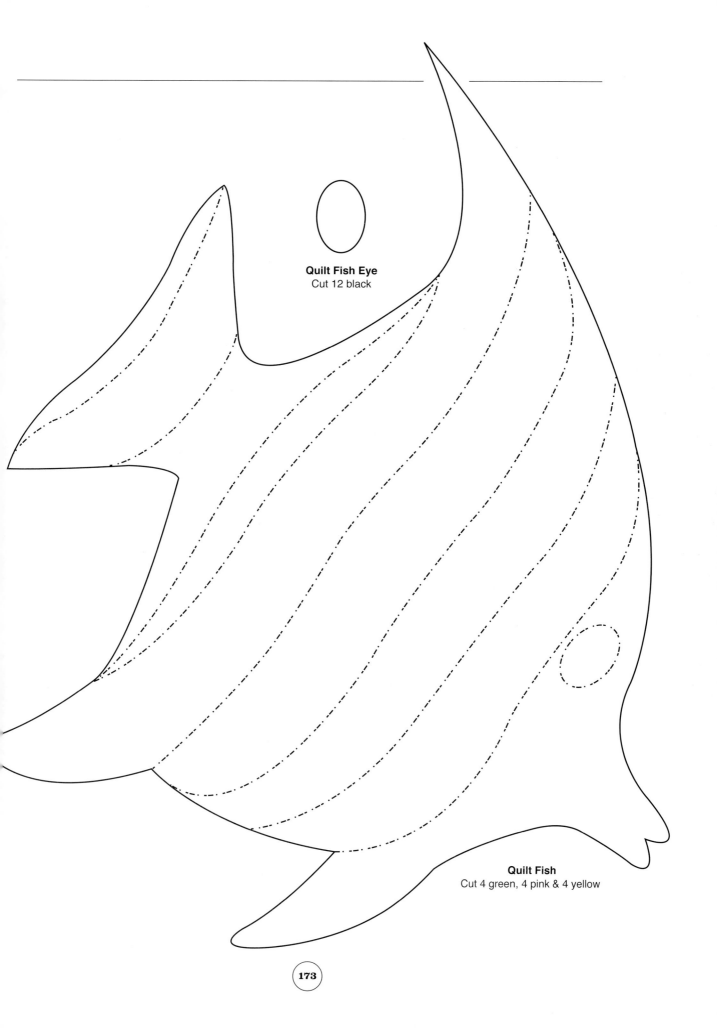

Quilt Fish Eye
Cut 12 black

Quilt Fish
Cut 4 green, 4 pink & 4 yellow

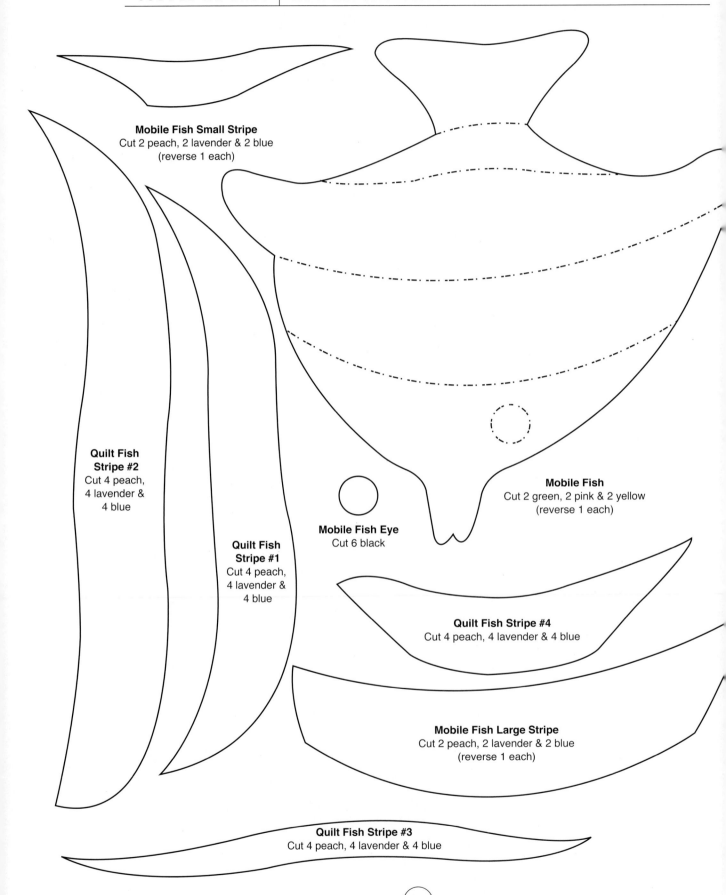

Mobile Fish Small Stripe
Cut 2 peach, 2 lavender & 2 blue
(reverse 1 each)

Quilt Fish Stripe #2
Cut 4 peach, 4 lavender & 4 blue

Quilt Fish Stripe #1
Cut 4 peach, 4 lavender & 4 blue

Mobile Fish Eye
Cut 6 black

Mobile Fish
Cut 2 green, 2 pink & 2 yellow
(reverse 1 each)

Quilt Fish Stripe #4
Cut 4 peach, 4 lavender & 4 blue

Mobile Fish Large Stripe
Cut 2 peach, 2 lavender & 2 blue
(reverse 1 each)

Quilt Fish Stripe #3
Cut 4 peach, 4 lavender & 4 blue

Fabric & Supplies

Page 18: *Split-Diamonds Pullover*—Kwik Sew pullover pattern #3001, David Textiles Nordic fleece fabric, and The Leather Factory Velvet Pigskin suede available from Tandy Leather

Page 20: *Royal Diamond Pintucks Jacket—McCall's* jacket pattern #2298, Valdani Threads variegated quilting thread, YLI Woolly Nylon, and American & Efird Mettler Metrosene Plus and Maxi Lock threads

Page 22: *Classy Beaded Top*—Simplicity jacket pattern #5970

Page 24: *Out 'n' About Jacket*— Simplicity jacket pattern #3299, David Textiles Nordic fleece fabric, Sulky Totally Stable iron-on tear-away stabilizer, Solvy water-soluble stabizer and rayon machine embroidery thread, and Prym Dritz Fray Check seam sealant

Page 26: *Border Print Pullovers & Hat*—Kwik Sew pullover and hat pattern #2817, David Textiles Nordic fleece fabric

Page 29: *Gold Braid Evening Vest*—Simplicity vest pattern #7320

Page 32: *Snips & Tucks Vest*—Simplicity vest pattern #9820

Page 36: *Sculpted Fleece Pajamas*—Kwik Sew pajama pattern #2907, David Textiles Nordic fleece fabric, Sulky Totally Stable iron-on tear-away stabilizer, Solvy water-soluble stabizer and rayon machine embroidery thread, and Prym Dritz Fray Check seam sealant

Page 40: *Red Tulip Pillow*—Thermo O Web HeatnBond Lite, Clover fusible bias, and Beacon Adhesives Fabri-Tac

Page 46: *Soft Sweet Shirt*—New Look shirt pattern #6976

Page 48: *White on White Evening Bag*— BagLady Press, Inc. gold purse chain and clasp, Kreinik #4 metallic braid, Thermo O Web HeatnBond Lite, and API Crafter's Pick Jewel Bond

Page 52: *Holiday Spirit Vest*—David Textiles Nordic fleece fabric

Page 54: *Jolly Holly Pillows*—David Textiles Nordic fleece fabric, and Fairfield Processing Corp. Soft Touch pillow forms

Page 57: *Festive Christmas Place Mats*—Fairfield Processing Corp. cotton batting, and API Crafter's Pick Fabric Glue

Page 68: *Snowflake Table Topper*—Marcus Brothers flannel fabric, and Hollywood Trims pompom fringe

Page 73: *Pumpkin Pullover*—David Textiles Nordic fleece fabric

Page 76: *Soft & Cuddly Bunny*—Simplicity pattern #9524

Page 80: *Eggs-ceptional Place Mats*—Robert Kaufman Zany for Zinnias flannel collection, Sally Houk Exclusives novelty yarn, June Tailor Fusible Batting, Beacon Adhesives Fabri-Tac, and Thermo O Web HeatnBond

Page 84: *Shimmering Strands Kimono*—Simplicity kimono pattern #7183, YLI Multi's Embellishment Yarn, YLI Candlelight Metallic Yarn, and American & Efrid Mettler Metrosene Plus and Maxi Lock threads

Page 86: *Dog's Stamp of Approval*—David Textiles Nordic fleece flannel, Kwik Sew dog coat pattern #2879, Thermo O Web HeatnBond and Fusible Vinyl and Pelle's Fabric Ink Pad, See Thru Stamps and Jacquard Textile Color provided by Purrfection Artistic Wearables

Page 88: *Teen Pajama Pants & Top*—Robert Kaufman flannel fabric, and Therm O Web HeatnBond Ultrahold fusible adhesive sheet and tape

Page 90: *Fluffy Fleece Bathrobe*—Kwik Sew bathrobe pattern #2727, David Textiles Nordic fleece fabric, and Fabric Café Chenille By The Inch, Cutting Guide and Chenille Brush

Page 97: *Autumn Leaves Throw*—Hobbs Thermore thin batting

Page 104: *Comfy Lounge Pillow*—Robert Kaufmann flannel fabric, and Fairfield Processing Soft Touch Polyester Fiberfill

Page 106: *Reversible Rug*—Therm O Web Quilter's Edge Ultra Hold iron-on adhesive tape

Page 108: *Woodsie Pines Window Set*—McCalls Flex-On Loops and Qwik-Tach Tape, RJR Fashion Fabrics Season in the Pines by Jean Wells, Pellon fusible nonwoven interfacing,

General Tools Mfg. Co. grommet kit #1260-4, OLFA Rotary Cutter and Omnigrid ruler and cutting mat

Page 114: *Snowflake Winter Warmer*—Kwik Sew hat pattern #2891, and David Textiles Nordic fleece fabric

Page 122: *Kid's Kimono*—New Look jacket pattern #6880 and API Crafter's Pick Fabric Glue

Page 124: *Baby Jacket Fun*—Kwik Sew jacket pattern #3127, David Textiles Nordic fleece flannel, and Fabric Café Chenille By The Inch, Cutting Guide and Chenille Brush

Page 136: *Flower Bright Jumper & Hat*—Simplicity pinafore/jumper pattern #9784

Page 139: *Nightie Night Giraffe Sleeper*—Simplicity sleeper pattern #5749 and API Crafter's Pick Fabric Glue

Page 133: *From Bag to Pad*—Warm & Natural cotton batting

Page 146: *My First Dollies*—Therm O Web HeatnBond fusible web

Page 153: *Barnyard Play Pad & Finger Puppets*—National Nonwovens Woolfelt

Page 161: *Baby's Cuddle Blanket*—Therm O Web HeatnBond

Page 166: *Sea Buddies*—DMC embroidery floss

Page 170: *Rainbow Fish Baby Quilt & Mobile*—Pellon Wonder Under fusible web

Contact Information

The following companies provided fabric and/or supplies for projects in Sew It Easy With Fleece & Flannel. If you are unable to locate a product locally, contact the manufacturers listed below for the closest retail or mail-order source in your area.

American & Efird, Inc.
www.amefird.com

API/The Adhesive Products Inc.
(510) 526-7616
www.crafterspick.com

Bag Lady Press, Inc.
www.baglady.com

Beacon Adhesives
(914) 699-3400
www.beacon1.com

Clover Needlecraft, Inc.
(800) 233-1703
www.clover-usa.com

David Textiles
(800) 548-1818

DMC Corp.
(800) 275-4117
www.dmc-usa.com

Dritz/Prim-Dritz Corp.
www.dritz.com

Fabric Café
www.fabriccafe.com

Fairfield Processing
(800) 980-8000
www.poly-fil.com

General Tools Mfg. Co.
www.generaltools.com

Hobbs Bonded Fibers
www.hobbsbondedfibers.com

June Taylor
(800) 844-5400
www.junetailor.com

Kreinik Mfg. Co. Inc.
(800) 537-2166
www.kreinik.com

Kwik Sew Pattern Co.
(612) 521-7651
www.Kwiksew.com

Marcus Brothers Textiles
(212) 354-8700
www.marcusbrothers.com

McCall's Patterns
www.mccallpatterns.com

National Nonwovens
www.nationalnonwovens.com

New Look Patterns
www.simplicity.com

OLFA
www.olfa.com

Pellon Consumer Products
(919) 620-7457
www.pellonideas.com

Purrfection Artistic Wearables
(800) 691-4293
www.purrfection.com

Robert Kaufman Fabrics
(800) 877-2066
www.robertkaufman.com

RJR Fabrics
www.rjrfabrics.com

Sally Houk Exclusives
(419) 347-7969

Simplicity Patterns
www.simplicity.com

Sulky of America
(800) 874-4115
www.sulky.com

Tandy Leather Company
(888) 890-1611
www.tandyleather.com

Warm & Natural/The Warm Company
(800) 234-9276
www.warmcompany.com

Therm O Web
(800) 323-0799
www.thermoweb.com

Valdani Threads
(866) 825-3264
www.valdani.com

YLI Corporation
(800) 296-8139
www.ylicorp.com

Special Thanks

We would like to thank the talented sewing designers whose work is featured in this collection.

Mary Ayres
Roll-Up Jewelry Pouch, 38

Lori Blankenship
Classy Beaded Top, 22
Reversible Drawstring Bag, 42
Snips & Tucks Vest, 32

Holly Daniels
Flannel Diaper Bag & Accessories, 142
Ready for Travel, 118
Star Overnight Backpack, 92

June Fiechter
Festive Christmas Place Mats, 57
Kid's Kimono, 122
Nightie Night Giraffe Sleeper, 139
Red Tulip Pillow, 40
Soft Sweet Shirt, 46
White on White Evening Bag, 48

Nancy Fiedler
Royal Diamond Pintucks Jacket, 20
Shimmering Strands Kimono, 84

Pearl Louise Krush
Sunshine Bright Throw, 100

Chris Malone
Flower Bright Jumper & Hat, 136

Connie Matricardi
Barnyard Play Pad & Finger Puppets, 153

Sheri McCrimmon
Soft Angelic Pair, 66

Patsy Moreland
Woodsie Pines Window Set, 108

Judith Sandstrom
Rainbow Fish Baby Quilt & Mobile, 170
Reversible Rug, 106

Carla G. Schwab
Flannel Message Center, 111

Bev Shenefield
From Bag to Pad, 133
Sea Buddies, 166

Marian Shenk
Fleur-de-lis Valentine Centerpiece, 70
Floral Lattice Pillow, 102
Gold Braid Evening Vest, 29
Soft & Cuddly Bunny, 76

Willow Ann Sirch
Autumn Leaves Throw, 97
Polar Pal Jacket, 126

Diana Stunell-Dunsmore
Baby's Cuddle Blanket, 171
Holiday Gift Bags, 60
My First Dollies, 146

Carol Zentgraf
Baby Jacket Fun, 124
Border Print Pullovers & Hat, 26
Comfy Lounge Pillow, 104
Dog's Stamp of Approval, 86
Eggs-ceptional Place Mats, 80
Fluffy Fleece Bathrobe, 90
Holiday Spirit Vest, 52
Jolly Holly Pillows, 54
Out 'n' About Jacket, 24
Pumpkin Pullover, 73
Sculpted Fleece Pajamas, 36
Snowflake Table Topper, 68
Snowflake Winter Warmer, 114
Split-Diamonds Pullover, 18
Teen Pajama Pants & Top, 88

Bibliography

Nancy Cornwell, Adventures in Polar Fleece.
Fairchild's Dictionary of Textiles.
Sara J. Kadolph, Anna Langford, Norma Hollen and Jane Saddler, Textiles.
Home Sewing Association Web site.